CONTESTED SOUTHERNNESS

The Linguistic Production and Perception of Identities in the Borderlands

JENNIFER CRAMER

Publication of the American Dialect Society 100

Supplement to *American Speech*, Volume 90

PUBLICATION OF THE AMERICAN DIALECT SOCIETY

Editor: ROBERT BAYLEY, *University of California, Davis*
Managing Editor: CHARLES E. CARSON, *Duke University Press*

Number 100
Copyright 2016
American Dialect Society
ISBN: 978-0-8223-6850-2

Library of Congress Cataloging-in-Publication Data

Names: Cramer, Jennifer. author.
Title: Contested Southernness : the linguistic production and perception of
    identities in the borderlands / Jennifer Cramer.
Other titles: Publication of the American Dialect Society ; no. 100.
Description: [Durham] : [Duke University Press], 2016. | Series: Publication of the
    American Dialect Society ; number 100 | "Supplement to American Speech,
    Volume 90."
Identifiers: LCCN 2016011320 | ISBN 9780822368502 (cloth : alk. paper)
Subjects: LCSH: English language–Dialects–Kentucky–Louisville. | English
    language–Dialects–Southern States. | Louisville (Ky.)–Languages. | Southern
    States–Languages. | Borderlands–Southern States.
Classification: LCC PE2927.L68 C73 2016 | DDC 427/.976944–dc23
LC record available at http://lccn.loc.gov/2016011320

British Library Cataloguing-in-Publication Data available

CONTENTS

ACKNOWLEDGMENTS

Growing up in Louisville, Kentucky, I always saw myself as a Southerner. No questions asked. But I often noted that many other Louisvillians had different visions of their own sense of regional belonging. When I moved to Indiana, and later to Illinois, I learned very quickly how varied people's perceptions of my Southernness were. Friends from New York, Minnesota, and the like were quick to point out just how Southern I sounded. On the other hand, every Tennessean, Alabaman, and Georgian I met declared with great confidence that there was no chance that I was a "real" Southerner. I started to wonder, every time I opened my mouth, how someone might view me. And so began my exploration of the place of Louisville in the regional dialect landscape of the United States.

While this book has my 2010 dissertation from the University of Illinois at its root, it is really a completely new endeavor, one that attempts to present a whole, well-rounded picture of the place of Louisville. From the earliest stages of dissertation writing to the culmination of this work in book form, I have received a great amount of love, support, and encouragement from so many people.

I would like to first thank Rakesh Bhatt for the countless hours spent helping me make this project a reality. He once told me that, in doing my research, I needed to do what I loved. I love being a Louisvillian. I love the way Louisvillians talk. I love how they talk about talk. Because of his encouragement, I embraced this project and have created something that I think other Louisvillians will love too. Thank you so much for being such a great advisor and mentor. For everything you have done for me, I am grateful.

But the project would not have gotten very far without the assistance of Dennis Preston. It was in his research program that I found a way to explore the questions I had about regional linguistic identities, and it was his expertise that led me to push the limits of what was being done at that time in the field of perceptual dialectology. He has encouraged me at every step of the project and has been instrumental in helping me get where I am today. Thank you for being so supportive, and I hope that you, as a fellow Louisvillian (basically), are proud of what I have accomplished.

I would also like to thank Eyamba Bokamba, Adrienne Lo, Marina Terkourafi, Margie Berns, Elaine Francis, and countless other mentors who have helped shape who I am as a linguist. I am so thankful for the encouragement and guidance you have provided me. As I have moved from student to scholar, I have found my colleagues at the University of Kentucky to be similarly supportive. I have been lucky to have the support of many members of the Linguistics Program here, especially Rusty Barrett and Andrew Hippisley, support that has helped me bring this book to completion.

For certain technical aspects of the project, I would also like to thank the nice people in the Geographical Information Systems (GIS) division of ATLAS at the University of Illinois and the GIS team in the Geography Department at the University of Kentucky, who helped with the preparation of the regional and state maps used in the data collection and with my understanding of how to use ArcGIS for my analyses. I also had help with the phonetics aspect of this project from the graduate student workers in the Illinois Phonetics and Phonology Lab, especially Shawn Chang, who provided a great deal of guidance in my use of Praat.

I also have several people to thank for their help in the collection and analysis of this data. The Kentucky map data was collected by students in a class called Language in Kentucky, offered at the University of Kentucky in fall 2011, in which those students were asked to go back to their hometowns (if in Kentucky) to get at least five people to draw maps and answer surveys. One linguistics student in that class, Nathan Hardymon, went on to pursue an undergraduate independent research project with me involving that data and was largely responsible for its digitization. Lindsey Austin, an undergraduate minor in linguistics at the University of Kentucky, helped collect the data regarding degree of difference, pleasantness, and correctness for an undergraduate independent research project in spring 2012. Finally, Ben Jones, my graduate student research assistant, has provided immense editorial and bibliographic assistance in the production of the book, which is highly appreciated.

The support of my colleagues in the Dissertation Discussion Group and the Language and Society Discussion Group at the University of Illinois was also greatly valued. In a similar vein, I would also like to thank the audiences from the 2009 and 2011 Linguistic Society of America annual meetings, the 2010 and 2014 American Dialect Society annual meetings, New Ways of Analyzing Variation 39 and 41, the Sociolinguistic Symposium 19, and the Southeastern Conference on Linguistics 78–81 for their helpful comments and suggestions on the presentation of this data.

The team at Duke University Press and my colleagues in the American Dialect Society have been immensely patient and helpful in the completion of this book. Thanks to Robert Bayley, who was persistent in asking me to submit my manuscript to the press and supportive of me as a young scholar navigating the world of book publishing. I would like to thank Charles Carson and two anonymous reviewers for their helpful insights as well.

Thanks also go out to all of my friends and family who have really been my strength throughout this whole process. You were all very encouraging and often provided me a chance to take a break from the stress of writing. I want to thank my parents for always supporting me and my career. I want to thank Isabelle, Nathan, and Benjamin for helping me learn how to play again and for being the shining lights in my life. You have been the ultimate motivation for finishing this book.

Last but certainly not least, I must thank my husband, Aaron. In addition to love and moral support, you provided invaluable technical support, which made my work a lot easier. You are awesome! I love you! This book is dedicated to you.

1. INTRODUCTION

A GREAT DEAL OF SCHOLARLY RESEARCH has addressed the issue of dialect mapping in the United States. Dialect mapping is the practice of dialectologists and sociolinguists aimed at defining dialect boundaries within a given area. These maps are typically created by grouping linguistic isoglosses, geographical boundaries for specific linguistic features, and are based on large survey projects where field-workers collect data about speakers' pronunciation or lexical inventory.

These studies are usually designed to present an overall picture of the dialect landscape. But what is often missing in these types of projects is an attention to the borders of a dialect region and to what kinds of identity alignments can be found in such areas.[1] This lack of attention to regional and dialect border identities is surprising given the salience of such borders for many Americans, as evidenced by, for example, the great success of Walt Wolfram's community-based research projects and documentaries in small, local communities like the Outer Banks, in larger regions like Southern Appalachia, and even among large ethnic communities like English-speaking Latinos across the United States.[2] This salience is often ignored by dialectologists, as nonlinguists' perceptions and attitudes have been generally assumed to be secondary to the analysis of "real" data, such as the phonetic and lexical variables used in traditional dialectology.

In this book, Louisville, Kentucky, is considered as a case study for examining how dialect and regional borders in the United States impact speakers' linguistic acts of identity (Le Page and Tabouret-Keller 1985), especially in the production of such identities, through the use or nonuse of certain linguistic features thought to be representative of said identities and in the perception of such identities, including both insider and outsider perceptions of the identities being produced by Louisvillians. According to Labov, Ash, and Boberg's (2006) *The Atlas of North American English*, Louisville is one of the northernmost cities to be classified as part of the South. Its location on the Ohio River, on the political and geographic border between Kentucky and Indiana, places Louisville on the border between Southern and Midland dialects.

In traditional dialectology studies, dialect borders, like those in Labov, Ash, and Boberg (2006), are usually depicted as being static, with a linguistic feature present on one side and absent on the other. Such a depiction lacks recognition of the fluidity and hybridity of identities that likely exists in the borderlands, and in Louisville, as in other third spaces (e.g., Bhabha 1994; Bhatt 2008), this fluidity of identities is exhibited through the linguistic production and perception of those identities that speakers claim.

Thus, the goal of this project is to show how these Louisville border residents categorize their own and other regional varieties of English, to examine how outsiders view the language and identities of people there, and to investigate the ways in which speakers produce and perceive the regional identities attributed to them. Through the examination of a variety of production and perception data, I show that the nature of identities at the border is neither simple nor straightforward. Louisvillians vary in their attitudes toward and production and perception of certain linguistic features in a way that indicates that they experience the border as the coming together of at least two distinct regions, one Southern and one non-Southern, seemingly choosing to align or disalign with different ones depending upon the interaction. Non-Louisvillians, on the other hand, view the urban center as the other in the largely rural state; at the same time, they perceive Louisville speech to be rather prestigious. Identity at the border, then, is shown to be fluid, complex, and dynamic, where speakers constantly negotiate, contest, and shift between identities, in the active and agentive expression of their amplified awareness of belonging brought about by their position on the border.

This project, then, not only adds to our specific understanding of the linguistic situation in Louisville, a rather understudied locale within sociolinguistics, but it also extends and expands our understanding of language and identity construction and the particular case of the effects of borders on such identities. In what follows, I situate this study in the realms of traditional dialectology, identity studies, border research, and perceptual dialectology and provide a short synopsis of the remainder of the book.

1.1. DIALECT MAPS AND FEATURES

There is a rather long history of dialect mapping in the United States. At least as early as the 1930s, the Linguistic Atlas of the United States and Canada was launched, and Hans Kurath took the lead in organizing the project (Chambers and Trudgill 1980, 17). It was divided into several regional surveys spanning several decades, including the *Linguistic Atlas of New England* (Kurath et al. 1939–43), Kurath's (1949) *A Word Geography of the Eastern United States*, Atwood's (1953) *A Survey of Verb Forms in the Eastern United States*, and, perhaps most famously, Kurath and McDavid's (1961) *The Pronunciation of English in the Atlantic States*. Kurath's work produced the map in figure 1.1, one of the earliest maps attempting to divide a small portion of the country into dialect areas.

Later works in the same tradition include the *Linguistic Atlas of the Upper Midwest* (Allen 1973–76), the *Linguistic Atlas of the Gulf States* (Pederson, McDaniel, and Adams 1986–92), and the *Linguistic Atlas of the Middle and South Atlantic States* (McDavid and O'Cain 1980), as well as the unpublished *Linguistic Atlas of the North Central States*, the *Linguistic Atlas of Oklahoma*, the *Linguistic Atlas of the Pacific West*, the *Linguistic Atlas of the Pacific North West*, and the *Linguistic Atlas of the Rocky Mountain States*. The Linguistic Atlas Projects, as they are collectively called, are currently maintained by Kretzschmar at the University of Georgia, and the image found in figure 1.2 represents the complete geographical scope of the projects.

These early studies were largely based on lexical inventories and the geographic distributions of specific words. Another project focusing on regional vocabulary is the *Dictionary of American Regional English* (*DARE* 1985–2013), which began in the 1960s and just recently came to comple-

FIGURE 1.1
Kurath's (1949) Word Geography of the Eastern States

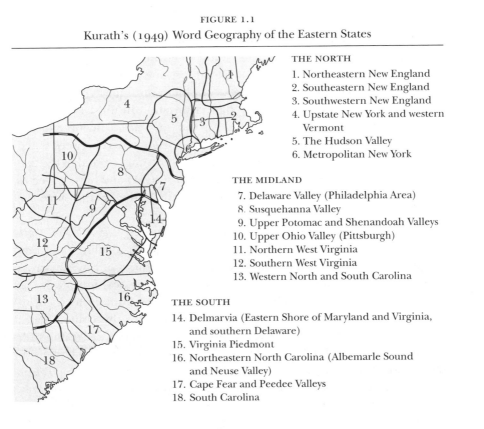

THE NORTH

1. Northeastern New England
2. Southeastern New England
3. Southwestern New England
4. Upstate New York and western Vermont
5. The Hudson Valley
6. Metropolitan New York

THE MIDLAND

7. Delaware Valley (Philadelphia Area)
8. Susquehanna Valley
9. Upper Potomac and Shenandoah Valleys
10. Upper Ohio Valley (Pittsburgh)
11. Northern West Virginia
12. Southern West Virginia
13. Western North and South Carolina

THE SOUTH

14. Delmarvia (Eastern Shore of Maryland and Virginia, and southern Delaware)
15. Virginia Piedmont
16. Northeastern North Carolina (Albemarle Sound and Neuse Valley)
17. Cape Fear and Peedee Valleys
18. South Carolina

FIGURE 1.2

Linguistic Atlas Projects Geographical Distribution (Kretzschmar 2004)

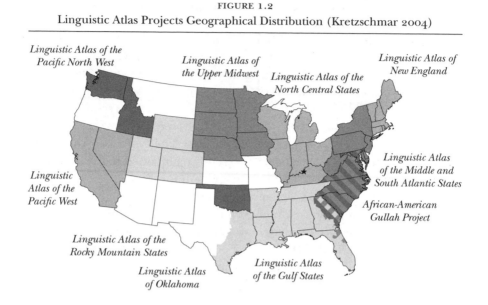

tion with the publication of the last print volume. This immense project included lexical and pronunciation data from all 50 states and has produced six print volumes in total, and a full electronic version is now available (http://www.daredictionary.com/). Carver (1987) used data from this project to produce the map in figure 1.3, which, until fairly recently, was the most commonly cited picture of dialect variation in the United States (Wolfram and Shilling-Estes 2006, 118). Carver's three major dialects, called North, South, and West, with small subdivisions therein, were based primarily on lexical data; however, these dialects also correspond to the patterns of vowel pronunciation presented in Labov (1991) and have served as the basic understanding of dialect divisions in the United States since the creation of Carver's map.

More recently, Labov, Ash, and Boberg published *The Atlas of North American English* (2006), a rather large-scale project providing "the first comprehensive view of the pronunciation and phonology of English across the American continent" (3). Instead of examining lexical inventories as had been the custom in traditional dialectology, the authors focused on phonetic variation in the language varieties present in the United States because, as they contend, the vowel patterns are what truly distinguish regional dialects of English in this country. Interviews primarily consisting of spontaneous speech and word lists were conducted via the Telsur project, a telephone survey carried out in the 1990s, which focused on area

FIGURE 1.3
Carver's (1987) Map of U.S. Dialects

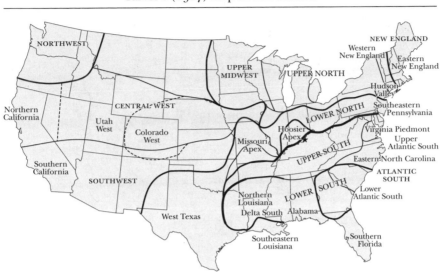

natives and their pronunciation patterns. The overall picture of the dialect landscape as determined by Labov, Ash, and Boberg (2006) is shown in figure 1.4.

As can be seen simply by comparing figures 1.3 and 1.4, dialectologists do not always agree on which lines to draw and how and where to draw them. For example, there has been some dispute about the existence of a Midland region, the appropriate divisions therein, and the durability of the boundaries, if they exist (cf. Kurath 1949; C.-J. Bailey 1968; Carver 1987; Davis and Houck 1992; Frazer 1994; Johnson 1994; Thomas 2010). Carver did not suggest the existence of a Midland, preferring instead to divide his North and South dialects into two main subsections: an upper part and a lower part. Carver's Lower North, however, corresponds well with Labov, Ash, and Boberg's Midland area, though the subdivision of the South from Carver's map is not the same as the divisions made in the Labov, Ash, and Boberg's South. These types of disagreements can affect how dialectologists classify particular parts of the country. One place where there seems to be a great deal of agreement is in the location of the northern boundary of the South. There is a long tradition of claiming that the Ohio River essentially serves as this northern border (i.e., Carver 1987; Labov 1991; Labov, Ash, and Boberg 2006). In Labov, Ash, and Boberg (2006), the line around the South, as seen in figure 1.4, has been drawn based on the pres-

FIGURE 1.4

Labov, Ash, and Boberg's (2006, 148) Map of North American Dialects

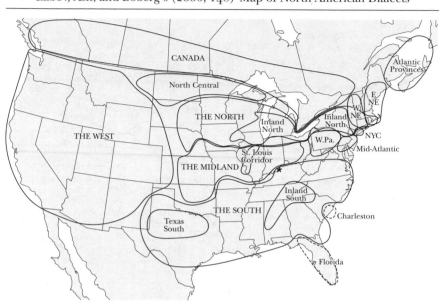

ence of a particularly Southern speech feature, monophthongization or glide deletion in the diphthong /aɪ/ in phonetic environments preceding voiced consonants (as in words like *ride*) and in open syllable contexts (as in words like *pie*). This line reaches just along the northern border of Kentucky, generally following the path of the Ohio River, as can be seen more clearly in figure 1.5.

The Ohio River, then, serves not only as the political and geographic border between Kentucky and Indiana, but also as the border between Midland and Southern speech. The arrow added to figure 1.5 indicates Louisville's location, just at the collision point of these two speech areas. An important caveat about Labov, Ash, and Boberg's atlas is that while it focused on the speech of individuals in urban settings, only one or two speakers were considered in most locations. The authors noted that it thus could not be considered an accurate description of the internal variation within a specific community and claimed that they hoped their work would "stimulate local studies to provide a more detailed view of the sociolinguistic and geographic variation in a given area" (3).

This call actually serves as one of the driving forces behind the current project. By examining the map in figure 1.5, it becomes clear that the positioning of Louisville as a Southern city, at least in terms of linguistic pro-

FIGURE 1.5
Labov, Ash, and Boberg's (2006) Boundary of the South

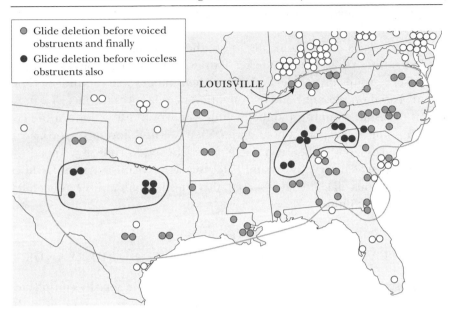

duction, seems somewhat arbitrary. Louisville is represented as a cluster of two points of different colors at the intersection of Southern and Midland dialects. The different colors for these two points indicate that one speaker exhibited the defining feature while the other did not. This difference in linguistic responses forces a reanalysis of the place of Louisville in the dialect map. In previous research examining the status of /aɪ/ in the speech patterns of Louisvillians (Cramer 2009), I showed that speakers' production often more closely matched speakers in the Midland dialect region and differed from the monophthongal pattern exhibited by Southerners. These results suggest that the situation on the isogloss border is more complicated than Labov, Ash, and Boberg suggest.

The position of Louisville is further complicated by the vague descriptions of the Midland dialect in the literature. Scholars often suggest that much of what is found in the Midland area is not unique to the region, claiming that all features found there are also found in the North or the South (Kurath and McDavid 1961). The area near the Ohio River in particular has been called a transition zone (Davis and Houck 1992; Johnson 1994), and it has been claimed that "[t]he lack of regularity in the Ohio Valley Midland is thus a simple reflection of the fact that the total Midland area is characterized as much by being not Northern and not Southern as it is by a body of uniform and universally used vocabulary" (Dakin 1971, 31). Therefore, a speaker in such a transitional position might be expected to produce some sort of identity that is Southern and, at the same time, non-Southern.

These facts depict Louisville as a rather complex locale for linguistic investigation. What is more, the act of drawing lines around areas, or more precisely, groups of people, and giving them names like "South" or "Midland" based on phonetic and lexical differences ignores the fact that those lines necessarily imply group belonging and group distinction. At the collision point of two dialect boundaries, then, we find border regions, areas portrayed as "zone[s] between stable places" (Rosaldo 1988, 85; Appadurai 1988, 19), which serve as dynamic sites for identity construction. In much of the previous dialectology research, this question of identity has been left relatively unexplored.

1.2. LANGUAGE, IDENTITY, AND THE BORDERLANDS

Linguistic studies of identity tend to focus on specific socially constructed categories like gender identity or nationality. The main assumption in the study of identity, particularly in linguistic anthropology, is that it is ultimately socially constructed (Bucholtz and Hall 2004). A structural perspective, one that assumes the static nature of identities, has been shown to be untenable (cf. Holmes 1997; Bucholtz 1999), and the current sociocultural perspective assumes that identities are dynamic and emerge within the context of an interaction "through the combined effects of structure and agency" (Bucholtz 1999, 209).

Bucholtz and Hall explain that "[i]dentity is the social positioning of the self and other" (2005, 586), making identity not only about an individual and how he or she is similar to some group. Identity also includes the ways in which we differentiate ourselves from others as well as the ways in which we describe others, which can often say more about the individual speaking than it does about the one being described (e.g., Galasiński and Meinhof 2002).

The question of how identities are constructed becomes quite complex when we consider what happens near borders, in the borderlands. While a border may simply be conceived of as a line (often a political or geographic boundary), the borderlands are considered to be strips of land on either side of the border (Bejarano 2006), "a region and set of practices defined and determined by this border that are characterized by conflict and contradiction, material and ideational" (Alvarez 1995, 448). Thus, in addition to being physical or geopolitical lines, borders can be conceived of as constructed by the communities under discussion, and the relevance of any given boundary can vary and change shape over time (Avineri and Kroskrity 2014).

These regions are locales for the convergence of political, social, and other identities (Flynn 1997). In these regions, identities are constantly challenged and transformed. Alvarez claims that borders and borderlands represent graphically the conflicts associated with the current organization of the world, adding, "For it is here that cultures, ideologies, and individuals clash and challenge our disciplinary perspectives on social harmony and equilibrium" (1995, 449).

Alvarez (1995) examines the history of borderland studies in anthropology. He claims that the anthropological investigation of borders grew out of many studies along the U.S.-Mexico border (e.g., Bustamante 1978; Hansen 1981; Stoddard, Nostrand, and West 1982) and that these studies provided the model for the study of other national borders. These researchers found interest in the U.S.-Mexico border because of its unique status as a boundary between the first and third worlds. These early studies were concerned mainly with issues of immigration. Later, anthropologists moved toward folklore and cultural products at the border as a way of investigating aspects of identity and cultural conflict. The field was further encouraged by native anthropologists challenging the traditional notions of subject and object in anthropological research, taking it upon themselves to investigate their own border communities from an insider's perspective. As more studies on this and other borders developed, the field of borderland studies quickly became a vibrant area of research.

The notion that borders serve as lines between distinct behaviors has been as pervasive in linguistic research as it has been in anthropological research. Traditional dialectology often focuses on drawing isoglosses, which suggest that distinct linguistic behaviors exist on either side of the line. But, if linguistic borders are anything like the borders studied by anthropologists (and they are), one might expect to find much more interesting behavior at the borders. Chambers and Trudgill (1980) turned their attention to one of these isoglosses to see whether the line actually served as a division between two distinct linguistic behaviors. Their focus was on a line between southern and northern England, where speakers vary in their pronunciation of ʊ/ʌ and a/ɑː. They suggest that areas around the isogloss, like borderlands, represent transition zones for the variables, where speakers exhibit variation in pronunciation.

Most linguistic or anthropological studies dealing with border identities have drawn on the situations found at national borders like, for example, the U.S.-Mexico border (e.g., Alvarez 1995; Bejarano 2006; de García 2006), the Uruguay-Brazil border (e.g., Carvalho 2006, 2010), or the Ireland–Northern Ireland border (Zwickl 2002), particularly in places where some rather large point of contention (i.e., immigration, language choice, religion) further separates the two nations. Bejarano (2006) examined the many distinctions in identity made by people at the U.S.-Mexico border (Latino, Chicano, Mexican, Mexican-American, etc.) that the majority of U.S. society ignores. Among her informants were both American-born and Mexican-born youths, who, in their identity creations, contested the relative Mexicanness or Americanness of their counterparts. She found that their identity positionings were tied up with their understanding of citizenship and the salience of linguistic choices. Participants were able to present their level of Mexicanness or Americanness based on both their birthright, so to speak, and their choice of English, Spanish, Spanglish, or code-switching between the languages. Bejarano emphasizes the contestation of identities that occurs in border communities, saying, "The borderlands thus is a place where people face simultaneous affirmations and contradictions about their identities" (22).

Some studies, though rather few, have examined the impact of regional borders on identities and identity construction. Llamas (2007), however, has demonstrated that a regional border can also serve as a dynamic site for identity construction and has done so through an examination of the linguistic practices in a community in England. In Middlesbrough, a city located on a regional and dialect border in Northern England, speakers not only vary in their production of linguistic variables, but also in their attitudes toward the varieties spoken nearby, such that a generational shift is evident in the construction of particular regional identities. Other studies, like Hazen's (2002) work in Warren County, North Carolina, present a focus on regional identities in the American context, which can aid linguists in the understanding of "how speakers conceive of themselves in relation to their local and larger regional communities" (241).

Attaining this understanding and recognizing that regions and their respective language varieties are of great importance to Americans is crucial to the study of regional linguistic variation. These issues are even more important when examining the borders of those communities. In this examination of Louisville, I consider the social facts of the city's place in the United States and attempt to present a picture of the perception and production of particular regional identities in light of such facts. Louisville's location on the Ohio River puts the city at numerous kinds of borders: political, geographic, linguistic, historical, cultural, and perceptual. As a border town, Louisville represents a location "where languages [dialects] are in contact, thus giving rise to issues of language use, ideology and attitude all intrinsically related to social, cultural and national identities" (Carvalho 2014, 1)—or for our purposes, regional identities—and it is likely that more than one regional identity is expressed by people in this city. As such, it will be necessary to address the complexity of mapping linguistic choices to identity construction in border towns in order to capture the sociolinguistic nuances of the language-identity interface.

The study of communities at borders serves to further our understanding of how borders impact linguistic variation and identity construction. It is not enough, however, to point to these external factors in creating an understanding of Louisville as a border town. It is important to discover whether people in Louisville recognize this border nature as well. As Johnstone (2004) noted, and Llamas (2007) made clear through her own study, understanding speaker ideologies is necessary for our understanding of identity alignments. One cannot simply assume that the border is salient for speakers without getting a sense of their attitudes about it, and it is in speaker's attitudes that one can discover ideological dispositions.

1.3. ATTITUDES, IDEOLOGIES, AND FOLK LINGUISTICS

Silverstein (1979, 193), in a seminal work, defined language ideologies as a "sets of beliefs about language articulated by users as a rationalization or justification of perceived language structure and use." Perhaps more simply, Kroskrity (2004, 498) defines them as "beliefs, or feelings, about languages as used in their social worlds." They are seen as imbued with the political, social, and moral issues prevalent within a community (Irvine and Gal 2000). Additionally, ideologies, like identities, are seen as dynamic entities, not static ones (Woolard 1992; Kroskrity 2004).

In studies of language ideologies, it becomes clear that individual speaker ideologies, particular linguistic forms, and specific social uses of these ideologies and forms are interconnected. Each one is thought to shape and inform the others, and within this triad, "language ideology is a mediating link between social structures and forms of talk" (Woolard 1992, 235). However, as Woolard (2008) has noted, it is quite difficult to focus on all three variables at the same time.

Perhaps this difficulty explains why previous dialectological studies were focused almost exclusively on linguistic variation, seeing attitudes as secondary, or as interesting parallel research. Variationist studies and language attitudes have often seemed to be separate ventures (Milroy 2004). This separation can be traced back to the early American structuralist tradition, particularly those scholars influenced by Bloomfield, who famously claimed that speaker ideologies only serve as distracters to genuine linguistic analyses (Bloomfield 1944). Milroy's (2004, 161) call for "a framework for incorporating into mainstream variationist work an account of language

attitudes, treated as manifestations of locally constructed language ideologies" encourages a move away from this structuralist perspective and toward
an understanding of the locally relevant social categories before beginning
linguistic research.

Folk linguistics is a framework of linguistic analysis that allows for a
comprehensive picture of linguistic variation of a place. This field has a
long history of connecting the ideologies of speakers to the realities of
linguistic variation. Despite the prevalence of the Bloomfieldian perspective for much of the mid-twentieth century, Hoenigswald (1966) incited
interest in the beliefs of speakers, or "the folk," in linguistic research. He
suggested that linguists should be concerned not only with language as production, but also with how people react to language and how people represent language in talk about language.

Perceptual dialectology is a branch of folk linguistics that has its focus
in what nonlinguists say about language and linguistic variation, including
where they think it comes from, where they think it exists, and why they
think it happens. It, too, has a long history, with some of its earliest roots in
the Dutch (Weijnen 1946; Rensink 1955) and Japanese (Sibata 1959) traditions. Research in modern perceptual dialectology, firmly rooted in the
research paradigm of Dennis Preston (e.g., Preston 1989; Preston 1999;
Long and Preston 2002), has produced a wealth of knowledge about language perceptions and production, and the tools of Preston's work utilized
in numerous American studies (e.g., Preston 1989; Benson 2003; Fridland,
Bartlett, and Kreuz 2005; Fridland and Bartlett 2006; Blake et al. 2008;
Bucholtz et al. 2007; Bucholtz et al. 2008; Evans 2011) have been used
around the globe to describe the views of nonlinguists (e.g., Coupland, Williams, and Garrett 1999; Demirci and Kleiner 1999; Kuiper 1999; Diercks
2002; Long and Yim 2002; Moreno Fernández and Moreno Fernández
2002; Romanello 2002; Montgomery 2007).

The tools used in these studies are varied, but certain tasks are rou-
tinely used in perceptual dialectology studies. One of the key ways in which
the folk beliefs of a population have been investigated involves the drawing
of a mental map of a location. A mental map, as a theoretical construct,
is conceived of as the image one has in his or her mind about a certain
place. Work in cultural geography (e.g., Gould and White 1986) has indicated that getting people to draw these maps can give us some insight into
how they see their world. Many perceptual studies have focused on nonlinguists' production of hand-drawn maps of regional dialectal variation in the
United States. In these studies, respondents are asked to draw lines around
areas on a blank map of the United States (or one with little detail) where
people "speak differently."[3]

An important focus in many folk linguistic studies is on how different a particular variety is perceived to be with respect to a respondent's own variety. For Preston, this task often involved having respondents rank each of the 50 states (plus Washington, D.C., and New York City) in terms of difference from how they speak. Additionally, participants rank the states and the two cities with respect to certain social characteristics, like the levels of pleasantness and correctness of the language variety spoken in a place.

Mental maps can give linguists clues about subjects' perception of space, which provides added ethnographic detail of the group under examination. Additionally, studies of folk beliefs can enhance our understanding of linguistic variation, in that it is unlikely that nonlinguists experience linguistic change in a way completely unrelated to the ways traditional dialectologists have described it (Niedzielski and Preston 2000).[4]

Work in perceptual dialectology has shown linguists why the perceptions of language users matter for linguistics. To express exactly why we need to consider folk beliefs in linguistic analyses, Preston (1993b, 252) has stated that

[w]ithout knowledge of the value-ridden classifications of language and language status and function by the folk, without knowledge of where the folk believe differences exist, without knowledge of where they are capable of hearing major and minor differences, and, most importantly, without knowledge of how the folk bring their beliefs about language to bear on their solutions to linguistic problems, the study of language attitudes risks being:

1) a venture into the investigation of academic distinctions which distort the folk reality or tell only a partial truth or, worse,
2) a misadventure into the study of theatrically exaggerated speech caricatures.

Without a clear understanding of the ways in which community members construct and perceive their own and others' languages and identities, we lose the important social and cultural information that informs our research. The borderlands serve as an area where these ideologies are particularly important in determining how speakers express belonging with respect to place.

While this book explores how real the border is for Louisvillians, some preliminary anecdotal evidence provides insight into the importance of this border in the imagination of many Louisvillians. For instance, when I asked Louisville participants about the position of Kentucky in the regional geography of the United States in a study on styles and stereotypes in the South (Cramer 2013), one participant exclaimed, "Man! We are just right on the border!" When prodded about Louisville's regional position, it has been my experience that University of Kentucky students, especially those from

Louisville, tend to be split on the city's relative level of Southernness. Additionally, numerous blogs, polls, news columns, and other forums online present varying positions on the question of Louisville's regional affiliation; for example, a poll at City-Data.com asked the question "Louisville, KY... southern or midwestern?" with the majority of people selecting Midwestern (City-Data.com 2007), while SkyscraperPage.com asked a similar question with the majority of responses pointing to Southern (SkyscraperPage.com 2008). Even more telling than the number of responses in these forums is the content of the posts, which further suggest the border experience of residents.

Utilizing the tools of perceptual dialectology will aid in our understanding of Louisville's place in the regional and dialectal landscape of the United States from the perspective of Louisvillians as well as from the perspective of outsiders. These tools will link the beliefs and attitudes of Louisvillians and non-Louisvillians to the realities of linguistic production in the city.

1.4. DATA AND METHODOLOGIES

The data analyzed in this book come from several different sources. Some of the primary data, which include the mental maps and language attitude surveys of 23 Louisvillians, most of who claim to have spent all or nearly all of their lives in the city, were collected in 2009. The participants in this part of the project were selected using the friend-of-a-friend method (Milroy 1980). As the data were collected outside of the context of the educational setting, it was not expected that participants had any formal training or knowledge about dialects or dialectal variation, though I did not ask this question. There were 10 female and 13 male respondents, ranging in age from 18 to 66. All participants were white native speakers of English. Individual and summary information about these participants is available in the appendix.

Following the models of mental mapping discussed in much of the folk dialectology research (Preston 1989, 1999), participants were given a physical copy of a map of a small region of the United States and were asked to draw lines around areas they consider to be dialect regions. The map used in this study can be found in figure 1.6.

Additionally, participants were asked to provide labels for the varieties they distinguished, and, after completion of the map, they were asked to complete a language attitudes survey about each variety they delimited. In this task, participants listed the labels used on their maps, and, using

FIGURE 1.6
Image Used for Mental Maps with Louisvillians

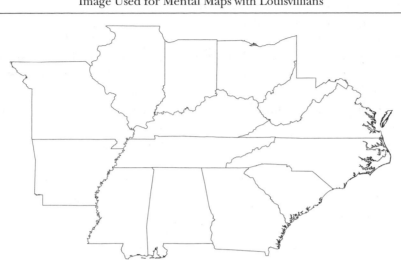

a four-point scale, rated these varieties in terms of the following social characteristics: difference (with respect to their own variety), correctness, pleasantness, standardness, formality, beauty, and education.[5] The survey featured 10 questions: 7 questions using this four-point scale and 3 open-ended questions dealing with other ways in which a particular variety might be described, the reasons for selecting a particular label, and the meaning behind the selected label. The questionnaire used can be seen in the appendix.

More recently, similar data were collected from people across the state. This data set comes from 250 Kentuckians and was collected by 37 undergraduate students in a course on Language in Kentucky in the fall of 2011. As part of an assignment, student researchers were instructed to go back to their hometowns and collect maps and language attitude surveys from at least five people age 18 or older.[6] Extra credit was given for students who collected more than five maps. Because of this collection method, many of the participants were relatives of the student researchers. It was again assumed that the participants had little or no expert knowledge about dialects, though this question was not explicitly asked. Instead, students were strongly discouraged from asking their friends from linguistics classes.

Participants ranged in age from 18 to 87. There were 135 female participants and 113 male participants, with 2 participants opting to omit their response to this question. Unlike the first survey of this sort, discussed above, these data include responses from nonwhite participants. While individual information about these participants would prove to be unwieldy for this book, I have provided summary information about all participants in this data set in the appendix.

The task in this project was the same as that described for the larger regional map, but participants were given a map of Kentucky only (figure 1.7), instead of the entire region (figure 1.6), requiring participants to consider more closely the variation that exists within the state itself. Perhaps because of the nature of data collection, not all maps generated by this task were usable. Some participants did not follow directions or the student researchers were not clear in providing assistance. Ultimately, 233 of the maps were deemed usable in this study and were analyzed following the procedures outlined below. While examinations of outliers in perceptual dialectology research has proven useful (Evans 2013), those maps are not presented or analyzed herein.

Once participants had completed the map drawing activity, they were once again asked to provide information regarding their language attitudes with respect to the regions they had delimited on their maps. The same questionnaire that was used in the regional study was used in this state-only study, and, as before, those questions can be found in the appendix.

To analyze the map data in these two data sets, each individual map was scanned and regions were digitized using ArcGIS, a tool that utilizes geographic information system (GIS) technology to connect the perceptual data to the world in which those perceptions are enacted. The goal in the analysis is to create a composite map featuring the most commonly delimited regional varieties. In selecting regions to digitize, I analyzed the specific labels used to determine which areas were most frequently used.

FIGURE 1.7
Image Used for Mental Maps with Kentuckians

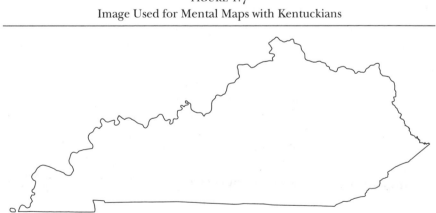

However, having free choice of labels, though a solid, bottom-up approach, presents analytical difficulty. How clear is it that "Southern" means the same thing in every map? Preston (1989) provided a template for hand-drawn maps, which aided in the conversion from individual maps and labels to a composite map. This template can be found in figure 1.8. Preston's template did not seem to encompass the entire spectrum of regions Louisvillians wanted to represent in the regional survey and was, perhaps obviously, even less useful with the Kentucky-only map. Thus, geography and frequency of occurrence were also considered in selecting which regions to represent in the composite maps. While the participants' original labels will be referenced when describing the nature of the varieties they delinieated, the composite maps use the overarching category labels used to analyze the language attitudes data.

Using the overarching category names as a starting point for the analysis of language attitudes, I examine how participants perceive the varieties of English they have delimited. Using statistical methods, specifically a post hoc Tukey HSD (Honestly Significant Difference) test, I compare the scores for different varieties to determine which varieties are perceived as better than or worse than others with respect to the social descriptors given in the language attitudes survey. More details about this test are provided in chapter 3.

FIGURE 1.8

Template for Choosing Labels in Hand-Drawn Map Activity (Preston 1989, 127)

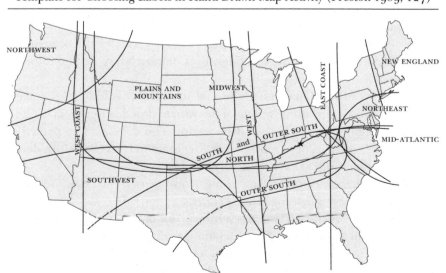

While these first two data sets use slightly adapted versions of the traditional tools of perceptual dialectology, additional data were colleted using
methodology found in much of the folk linguistic research: rating the 50
states, Washington, D.C., and New York City in terms of degree of difference, level of pleasantness, and level of correctness. These data were taken
from 68 Kentuckians in an online survey, which employed Qualtrics survey
software, conducted with the help of an undergraduate research assistant
in the spring of 2012 as part of an independent study. In this survey, participants were asked to rate each state and the two cities on a scale of 1–10
for correctness and pleasantness and a scale of 1–4 for degree of difference (following the methodology of Preston's early work, as summarized in
Niedzielski and Preston 2000). In these scales, a lower response indicated a
lower level of agreement (i.e., less different, pleasant, or correct).

As with the map drawing activity, it was assumed (though not verified)
that participants would have little or no technical background in the study
of dialects. Participants ranged in age from 18 to 80 and represented many
different parts of the state, including 8 respondents who claimed to be from
somewhere other than Kentucky. In total, 21 males and 47 females participated. Only 2 participants indicated a race/ethnicity other than white.

The demographic survey was slightly different for this data set. Participants were given more freedom to describe their demographic categories
(i.e., questions were open-ended), which meant the student researcher and
I had to define how to group participants in the initial analysis of the data.
For instance, based on the city reported as his or her hometown, each participant was placed in a region of Kentucky, with Louisville set apart for
the current analysis. This survey also explored whether the participants'
perceptions of themselves having a "Southern accent" (by self-report)
impacted the ratings given to each state. Summary data for the participants
in this survey (based on these variations in demography) can be found in
the appendix.

In terms of data analysis, traditional statistical methods (e.g., means,
ANOVAs, *t*-tests) are used to determine which varieties Kentuckians hold
in high esteem and which ones they do not. The data are also presented
in graphical form, using choropleth maps created in ArcGIS. More details
about these methods are found in chapter 3.

Finally, the production data come from an original SOAPnet[7] reality television show, *Southern Belles: Louisville* (2009). The short-lived show,
described as a "docusoap" or "docudrama," follows the lives of five Louisville women in their 20s and 30s, detailing their experiences as friends, as
professionals, and as bachelorettes. It is a typical reality show, with segments
of free conversation, long stories, and monologues, also known as "con-

fessionals," spoken directly into camera.[8] These women form a group of friends, very involved in different aspects of life in Louisville.

The show premiered May 21, 2009 and aired only 10 episodes, concluding on July 23, 2009. SOAPnet's press release describes the show as follows:

"Southern Belles: Louisville" is a real-life "Sex and the City" that takes place in the South, but not the South that stereotypes are made of. The backdrop is the progressive, art-centric and warm community of Louisville, Kentucky. The series will showcase the intense friendships and family values that are part of the Southern way of life. These five contemporary and independent women are all at critical crossroads in their lives: Some are confronting their biological clocks, some are still looking for Mr. Right and are trying to find their career paths, and one is preparing for her wedding. [SOAPnet 2009]

Thus, the show is positioned as being representative of the South, and as such, one might expect the women to also be appropriate representatives. Also, positioning Louisville as Southern, using stereotypical notions of warmth and family values, yet somehow non-Southern, depicting the city as art-centric and progressive, with the implication that these characteristics are not stereotypically associated with the South (despite a history of both phenomena in the South), adds to our understanding of Louisville as a border city.

Below I describe each of the five women who star in the show. These descriptions are based on my own ethnographic understanding of the women in watching and transcribing the show.

Emily, the youngest member of the group, is the daughter of rather religious parents, including an overprotective father who owns his own company. Her parents want her to get involved with the family business, but Emily would rather pursue her own dream of becoming a television reporter, specializing in entertainment news. Her main focus during the show is whether to move to Las Vegas for an opportunity in television, despite her family's wishes for her to stay in Louisville.

Hadley is characterized as the "girl next door," who has a penchant for "bad boys." She cannot seem to decide what she wants in life; she began a Ph.D. but decided to take a break from school to work as a personal assistant. The show follows Hadley's adventures in dating and deciding on a career path.

Julie, the oldest and only African American member of the group, is a model who discovers that her career must change course because of her age. She must now look for roles for older women. She is single, which she claims is caused by her devotion to her career. Julie wants a husband and a family but fears she may be short on time. In the show, the audience sees her battle with juggling a career and a dating life.

Kellie, like Julie, feels the pressure of time. She is 32 and has already been divorced twice. She desperately wants children, but the man she is dating during the course of the show does not want children. The show deals extensively with how Kellie will resolve this issue. During the show, the audience comes to understand the many trials Kellie has struggled through in her life: two divorces, a miscarriage, an eating disorder, a drug addiction, and a complicated early family life.

Shea, the daughter of a wealthy Louisville doctor, is portrayed as spoiled and snobbish. She is and wants to continue to be a part of Louisville's high society. Her fiancé, however, does not share the same background. The show chronicles their courtship. Throughout the show, the audience sees Shea's desire for expensive things, which makes her fiancé nervous about their lives together. The focus is on Shea's desire to get married right away.

Overall, the characters are similar in many ways, but differ in some: Shea comes from money, while Kellie had married into money and lost it in the divorce. Hadley is portrayed as not having a lot of money, though she still gets to enjoy some of the pleasures of high society by having these friends. Their ages range from 24 to 34, a rather large range for a small group of friends. Yet the show insists that these women are life-long friends, with traditions and a history. The show features interactions between all five women, as well as subplots involving individuals and smaller groups, perhaps indicating that certain relationships are more cemented. A summary of the ethnographic data about these women, gleaned from a press release (SOAPnet 2009), as well as my viewing of the show, is presented in table 1.1.

For the analysis of the production of identity, I examined the production data for specific phonetic features typically associated with Southern dialect areas, including the Southern Vowel Shift (SVS) (see Fridland 1998, 2001; Labov, Ash, and Boberg 2006) and the front lax prenasal merger (the PIN/PEN merger) (see G. Bailey 1997; Labov 1996; Labov, Ash, and Boberg 2006; Thomas 2008), as well as for one feature that seems to be resisted in Southern speech, namely the low back vowel merger (the COT/CAUGHT merger) (see Frazer 1996; Gordon 2006; Labov, Ash, and Boberg 2006; Irons 2007). The vowel classes under investigation include /aɪ/, /eɪ/, /ɛ/, /i/, /ɪ/, /u/, and /oʊ/ for the SVS; /ɛ/ and /ɪ/ in prenasal position for the PIN/PEN merger; and /ɔ/ and /ɑ/ for the COT/CAUGHT merger. Additionally, tokens for /æ/ and /ʌ/ were included as control vowels in the analysis of the SVS. These vowels are thought to participate minimally, if at all, in the SVS, making them potentially stable vowels. These stable vowels were used to measure the general patterns of movement for the vowels involved in the shift, providing a reliable evaluation across speakers.

TABLE 1.1

The "Southern Belles" of SOAPnet's *Southern Belles: Louisville* (2009)

Name	Age	Race	Further Information
Emily	24	Caucasian	Father owns a business; would rather be a television reporter
Hadley	26	Caucasian	"Girl next door"; trouble with career and dating life
Julie	34	African American	Career as a model; has been cautious in love and career
Kellie	32	Caucasian	Divorced twice; married into money; frank and honest
Shea	28	Caucasian	From wealth; seen as snobbish; wants to marry now

The claim is that the presence or absence of particular linguistic features serves as an index of certain linguistic identities. Therefore, I present an acoustic analysis of the speech of each of the five women, discussing in detail which linguistic features are present and which are absent in each woman's speech.

The data consist of more than seven hours of broadly transcribed video taken from this television series, and the complete transcript served as a corpus of vowel tokens. For the SVS, a program was designed to randomly select words in the transcript that featured one of the vowels under analysis, using *dictionary.com* as a database for anticipated ("standard") pronunciations. When words were randomly drawn that could not be located in the dictionary, they were judged by the author (e.g., *bootylicious*). In cases where there were two possible tokens of the same vowel class in one word, I used a coin flip to determine which vowel to analyze. For each subject, a word was used only once per vowel class, so as to avoid duplication of the same exact token, which, because of television editing processes, was quite possible. Plurals, homophones, and contractions, thus, were not considered to be the same word. For the /aɪ/ vowel tokens, prevoiceless environments were not used, since monophthongization is less likely in these environments. Also, words like *a*, *the*, and *and* were not used as tokens because of the reductive nature of such words in natural speech. Finally, the word *Louisville* was rejected as a candidate because of the issues associated with the pronunciation of the city's name.[9]

For the mergers, following Hazen (2005), vowel tokens were extracted from single syllable words wherein the vowel under investigation appeared in noninitial position before [n] or [m] (for the PIN/PEN merger) or before [t] or [k] (for the COT/CAUGHT merger). In all, at least ten tokens were selected for each of the vowel classes under investigation for each subject, for a total of 110–15 target tokens per speaker.[10] For the SVS, five tokens for each of the control vowels were also collected, ultimately resulting in 115–20 total tokens per speaker.

Each target word was subjected to spectral analysis using Praat (various versions; for the most recent version, see Boersma and Weenink 2015). For each word, I hand-selected the vowel in Praat through visual inspection of the spectrogram. The boundaries of the vowel were determined by listening to the speech sample, zooming into the spectrogram, looking for the higher energy bands typical of vowel formants, and identifying the end of the preceding phoneme and the closure of the following phoneme. This type of acoustic analysis is necessary and better than traditional methods of transcription, especially when the analyst is a member of the speech community under examination, because, as Feagin noted, "It is particularly difficult for a member of that speech community to hear local vowels as being different from the standard vowel charts" (1986, 90). More detailed information about the analysis of each vowel class can be found in chapter 6.

Considering the project as a whole, it is expected that these many types of data can provide the most complete picture of how Louisvillians view their own variety, how they view the varieties of others, how others view the varieties spoken in Louisville, and how those perceptions do or do not line up with facts of production. My approach to research is multidimensional, drawing insights from many theoretical traditions, including those from the fields of linguistics, anthropology, psychology, and sociology. I use methods from folk linguistics, anthropological studies of borderlands, and traditional phonetic and sociolinguistic analyses to present a precise analysis of speakers' identity positionings in and of Louisville.

1.5. MOVING FORWARD

This book presents a picture of regional identity in Louisville that is chaotic and confused. It begins, in chapter 2, by considering the messy social facts of Louisville's location at many kinds of borders. The chapter serves to demonstrate how Louisville is located in the borderlands, positioned between two worlds, one Southern, one not, by presenting a discussion of the specific geopolitical, sociohistorical, linguistic, perceptual, and cultural situation present in the city. The description of Louisville as "a place between places" (Llamas 2007) provides support for the investigation of linguistic practices and language attitudes in this particular borderland. It is because of Louisville's position, history, and cultural confusion that one can expect to find interesting insights into general identity construction and the more specific effects of borders on identity positionings through an examination of linguistic practices.

To better understand how Louisvillians experience their own regional identity, it is important to recognize how Louisvillians see the dialect landscape of the United States in general. Chapter 3 portrays some of the broader beliefs Louisvillians have about language variation. The data explored in this chapter (correctness and pleasantness ratings of the states and two cities, regional and state-only individual and composite maps, and language attitude data from the regional and state-only surveys) reveal how Louisvillians understand and label regional varieties of English spoken in the United States, what attitudes they have toward those ways of speaking, and how these impressions are realized through stereotypes and generalizations. To examine Louisvillians' folk perceptions of dialectal variation, the data examined in chapter 3 include not only the mental maps they draw, but also the labels they employ for the varying dialects of English they distinguish and their attitudes toward different varieties.

More specifically, however, this book is concerned with where Louisvillians see themselves as belonging. The regional linguistic identity of Louisville from the perspective of Louisvillians is presented in chapter 4, which locates Louisville within this broader dialect landscape, showing how Louisvillians view the specific language situation in their own city. To know if Louisvillians see their categorizations of Louisville as appropriate, I explore speakers' ideologies about the different categories they depict. Since the premise of the book is that Louisville is positioned at a border, chapter 4 also addresses whether Louisvillians represent this same border nature in their placement of Louisville in the dialect landscape of the United States and in their attitudes toward their own speech. The maps and attitudes data explored in this chapter are the same as those encountered in chapter 3, with the focus turned on the placement of Louisville in the dialect landscape. This chapter also includes an examination of the degree of difference data from the ratings of the 50 states, Washington, D.C., and New York City.

However, because identity is about the self and the other (Bucholtz and Hall 2005), it is not enough to suggest Louisville's regional identity positionings based on the perspectives of insiders alone. In chapter 5, data from other Kentuckians and a few non-Kentuckians are presented to show where outsiders think Louisville belongs. The data in this chapter include the correctness, pleasantness, and degree of difference ratings of the 50 states, Washington, D.C., and New York City and the state-only maps and language attitudes data of non-Louisville participants. While Louisville has been painted as being located on a border, in actuality, it is likely that the entire state is located at a border (Cramer 2012). This chapter explores how other Kentuckians distinguish themselves from Louisvillians not only by looking at the broader dialect landscape of the United States, but also by examining the specific distinctions made within the state.

Once the on-the-ground categories for labeling and discussing regional linguistic identities have been established, the realization of these categories through linguistic means can be examined. Chapter 6 connects the beliefs of Louisvillians and non-Louisvillians about regional identity to the production of certain linguistic variables associated with different regional varieties of English by exploring the production data described above. This chapter identifies how well the categorizations made by nonlinguists match up to those made by dialectologists. Specifically, because dialect maps often position Louisville as part of the Southern dialect region, we must examine production data for elements of Southern speech.

Finally, chapter 7 brings together the facts presented in the previous chapters to depict regional identity at the borders as very fluid and complex. I summarize the results of the overall project, indicating how identity alignments in the borderlands are neither simple nor straightforward. Instead, identities in these areas are constantly contested and always in contention, and the speech patterns of people from the area reveal their split identities.

It is my hope that, by exploring certain questions about language and identity in regional borderlands, the answers will not only help us better understand the specific linguistic situation in Louisville, a rather understudied location, but also provide some insight into the dynamic nature of linguistic (and other) borders, pointing specifically to the ways in which identity work is interactionally located and ideologically produced in the space between relatively stable dialect areas. That is,

[w]ithin a language ideology framework, speakers' own comments about language and other social phenomena are used as a means of interpreting and understanding linguistic variation in the community, thus allowing insight into social psychological motivations for sociolinguistic differences that may be otherwise inaccessible to the analyst. [Llamas 2007, 581]

This book reveals that people in Louisville do not have a uniform way of classifying their city in terms of regional identity. This lack of uniformity suggests that Louisvillians see themselves as located at a border or at the intersection of at least two cultures in the dialect landscape of the United States. Louisvillians appear to be constantly contesting and negotiating the identities they attribute to themselves and those attributed to them by others. They seem to shift in and out of regional identities with ease, producing both Southernness and non-Southernness in their linguistic production and perception of identities.

2. BETWEEN TWO WORLDS

Since the main objective of this book is to gain a better understanding of the ways in which regional identity is perceived and constructed linguistically at borders, it is crucial to begin by using specific facts to situate Louisville as a border city. I begin by providing some general information about the city, including maps of the city itself and the city in its larger geographic region. This physical locating of Louisville is followed by detailed discussions of the ways in which Louisville can be considered as "a place between places" (Llamas 2007), examining how geographic, political, linguistic, historical, cultural, and perceptual facts position Louisville as Southern and yet non-Southern simultaneously.

2.1. GENERAL INFORMATION

Louisville, home to the world-famous Churchill Downs and the annual running of the Kentucky Derby, the Louisville Slugger baseball bat, and Muhammad Ali, was founded by George Rogers Clark in May 1778, when he established "the remotest outpost of American settlement during the War for Independence" (Share 1982, 3) at Corn Island, near present-day Louisville. The city was named in honor of King Louis XVI of France. The city "is located on the left bank of the Ohio River about six hundred miles downstream from the confluence of the Monongahela and Allegheny Rivers at Pittsburgh" (Kleber 2001, 334). Louisville is bounded by the Ohio River to the north and west.

As the metropolitan area, by some accounts, includes parts of southern Indiana (i.e., Jeffersonville, New Albany, and Clarksville), the entire area is often referred to as *Kentuckiana* (Louisville Metro Government 2009).[1] The map in figure 2.1 shows Louisville's position in the surrounding region.

With a population of nearly 750,000, according to the 2010 census, Louisville is the largest city in Kentucky, a fact that has been true since 1830, when Louisville surpassed Lexington as the dominant urban center in the state (Share 1982). This number includes both the inner-city and the suburban populations, since the Louisville and Jefferson County governments merged in 2003 to become Louisville Metro, one of the 20 largest cities in the country (Louisville Metro Government 2009). Indeed, in a largely rural state, Louisville is singularly marked as the state's only Class 1 city (Kentucky League of Cities 2011).[2]

FIGURE 2.1

Louisville within Its Larger Region

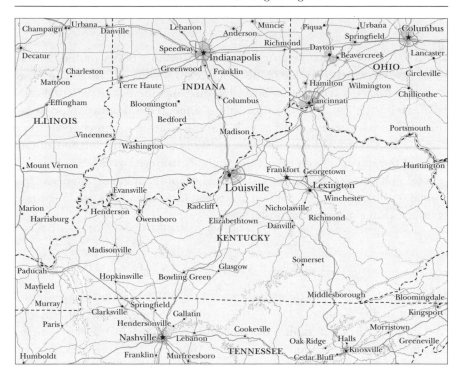

Descriptions of Louisville's location in the landscape of the United States vary, though it is often positioned just south of a North-South regional border in the United States. The city has been called "America's southernmost northern city and its northernmost southern city" (Emporis .com 2015). Another description takes geography as the starting point, but turns to other explanations in pointing out the complex nature of regionality in the area:

In a larger geographic sense, Louisville lies at the western limits of the Outer Bluegrass physiographically, and, as a town, between the Midwest and the South culturally. This latter situation was reinforced by a large electric sign that was located for many years at the southern end of the Clark Memorial Bridge on the Louisville Gas and Electric Power Plant proudly proclaiming Louisville as the "Gateway to the South." [Kleber 2001, 335]

However, other sources emphasize Louisville's strong connection to the Midwest. Meyer (1989), in his discussion of manufacturing growth in the

Midwest, categorized Louisville as one of its 20 largest industrial cities in 1880. America 2050, the Regional Plan Association's (2013) infrastructure program, situates Louisville as part of a Great Lakes megaregion, which groups the city with major Midwestern cities like Detroit, Pittsburgh, Cleveland, and Chicago. These kinds of depictions, as well as other geographical, political, linguistic, historical, cultural, and perceptual facts point to Louisville's position as a border town.

2.2. AT A GEOGRAPHIC AND POLITICAL BORDER

Historically, geographical borders served as barriers to contact between people. Mountains and rivers provided natural protection from outside influences, good or bad. In a more connected, more mobile, globalized world, perhaps this role for geographical borders is outdated. But the history of geographic borders points to some of the reasons why certain borders have had great significance in particular areas.

In Louisville, the Ohio River served as the reason for its founding (e.g., Kleber 2001). The Falls of the Ohio, the only natural barrier to navigating the Ohio River, is situated in the river where present-day Louisville is located. In the time of its founding, it was at this location that "[t]he river dropped twenty-two feet in a distance of two miles, making passage dangerous at high water and all but impossible most of the year" (Share 1982, 3). River traffic was brought to a halt in this area, though locals were able to help in navigation by unloading and moving boats downriver. Eventually, canals and the McAlpine Locks and Dam were built to facilitate navigation, but by that time, Louisville had already established itself as an important river town and major shipping port.

Some of the most natural political borders are also geographic. In this case, the Ohio River serves as the political boundary between Kentucky and Indiana as well, though as maps indicate, most of the river is actually within Kentucky's state borders.[3] This geographic and political border, however, can, in some ways, be seen as having little real importance today. For instance, many residents of Southern Indiana find work in Louisville, and vice versa. In 1990, more than 32,000 workers came from Indiana for jobs in Louisville (Yater 2001). Additionally, the two states have recently come together in attending to the traffic needs of the larger metropolitan area by developing the Louisville–Southern Indiana Ohio River Bridges Project (2013).

Beyond state boundaries, one might consider the regional divisions set out by the United States Census to be another type of political boundary.

FIGURE 2.2

Census Regions and Divisions of the United States

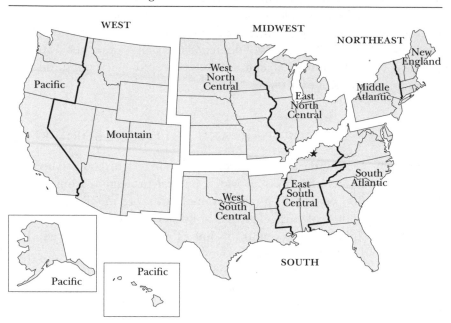

In dividing the country into four divisions, the Ohio River again serves as the dividing line between what is called "South" and "Midwest," as seen in figure 2.2.

Another official federal designation for Kentucky, as defined by the U.S. Office of Management and Budget (1974), places the state in Region IV, along with other Southeastern states like Alabama, Florida, and the Carolinas, as seen in figure 2.3. Similarly, as can be seen in figure 2.4, the U.S. Bureau of Economic Analysis (2011) classifies Kentucky in the Southeastern region when making comparisons of economic data. Again, the Ohio River forms part of the northern boundary of this region.

These numerous official regional designations indicate the importance of the Ohio River in the larger geopolitical realm of the United States. Whether the division is made in terms of individual state sovereignty, as in the case where the river separates Kentucky and Indiana, or in terms of economic and other federal-level comparisons, the Ohio River serves as the dividing line. As such, Louisville, as a river town, as well as the rest of the state, is situated just south of this important line.

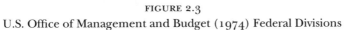

FIGURE 2.3
U.S. Office of Management and Budget (1974) Federal Divisions

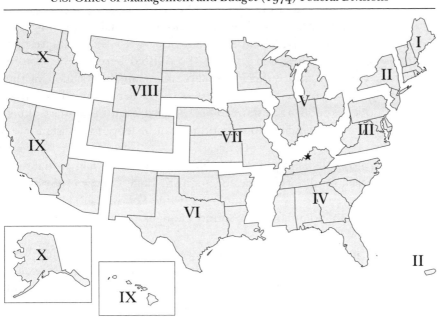

FIGURE 2.4
U.S. Bureau of Economic Analysis (2011) Regional Map

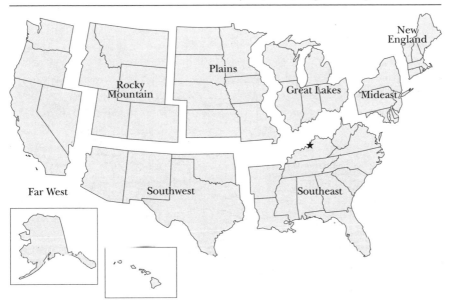

2.3. AT A LINGUISTIC BORDER

As noted in chapter 1, there is a long tradition of using some part of the Ohio River as the northern border of the Southern dialect region (e.g., Carver 1987; Labov 1991; Labov, Ash, and Boberg 2006). An interesting comparison of the earliest and latest of those listed here can be seen in figure 2.5. Here, we find rather close agreement on the location of the northern boundary of the South, at least as it concerns Louisville. Labov, Ash, and Boberg (2006, 149) state, "The Midland/South boundary along the Ohio River also coincides for a good part of its length with the Lower North/Upper South boundary of Carver."

What is most interesting about the similarities in these maps is that they were each based on different types of linguistic data. Carver (1987) used lexical inventories to draw his boundaries, while Labov, Ash, and Boberg (2006) base their boundaries on sound changes occurring in different parts of the country.

Another linguistic way of determining where Louisville belongs is to examine specific linguistic features associated with the region. For example, a fairly well-recognized feature of Southern speech is what linguists call

FIGURE 2.5
Carver (1987) and the *Atlas of North American English*
(Labov, Ash, and Boberg 2006, 150)

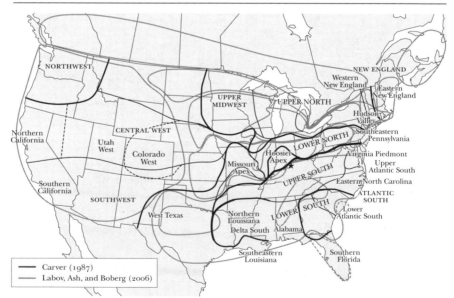

the front lax prenasal merger, which causes Southerners to pronounce the word *pen* as homophonous with *pin*. The map in figure 2.6, taken from the Labov, Ash, and Boberg (2006, 150), shows where speakers have this feature, and Louisville is located in the region of Kentucky where the merger is not found.

On the other hand, at least according to the Labov, Ash, and Boberg (2006), Louisvillians also do not have a feature common in the Midwest and West but typically avoided by Southerners, namely the low back vowel merger, which causes many people to pronounce *cot* and *caught* in the same manner. The map in figure 2.7 shows that, again, Louisvillians do not exhibit this feature.

This lack of regionally attributed features suggests that Louisville is located in a linguistic no-man's-land. As we will see in chapter 6, however, it is not clear that Louisvillians lack both mergers; instead, like with Hazen's (2005) work in West Virginia, both mergers seem to be present, but to varying degrees. I argue that the use or nonuse of these features allows Louisvillians to make connections to both identities.

Research on the linguistic variation specifically present in Louisville has been minimal, though what has been conducted further reveals this

FIGURE 2.6
PIN/PEN Merger (Labov, Ash, and Boberg 2006, 150)

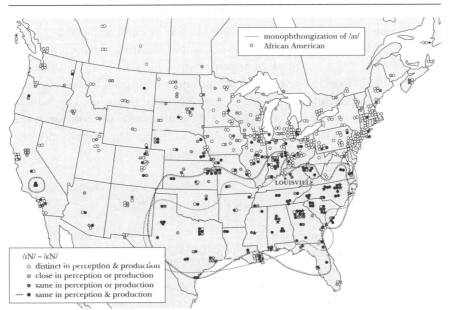

FIGURE 2.7
COT/CAUGHT Merger (Labov, Ash, and Boberg 2006, 150)

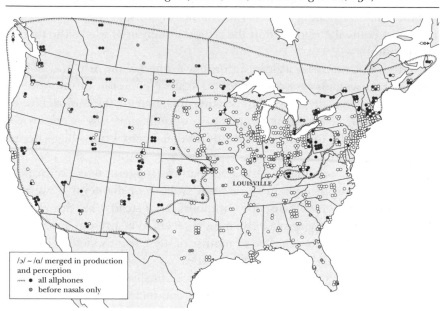

border nature. Howren, whose 1958 dissertation is the only major linguistic research undertaking on Louisville prior to this work, described Louisville's vocabulary as having North and South Midland tendencies, while squarely positioning Louisville as (South) Midland (as opposed to Southern) with respect to phonology, despite his participants exhibiting the monophthongal variant of /aɪ/, a hallmark of Southern speech. When explicitly testing how Louisvillians identified regionally and quantifying such identifications with /aɪ/ monophthongization, Miller (2008) found that while Louisvillians equally choose the label Midwestern and Southern for identification purposes, those who self-identified as Southern were more likely than the other group to utilize this marker of Southern identity.

2.4. AT A HISTORIC BORDER

The history of Louisville's border nature begins at least as early as the Revolutionary War, when explorers were trying to find the best ways to move westward. It has been noted that "[t]he first and principal portion of the Kentucky pioneers—those who fought the Revolutionary battles—entered Kentucky by the Cumberland Gap route" (Hulbert 1903, 176), which is located in the southeastern portion of the state, where Kentucky, Tennessee, and Virginia meet. The Ohio River served this function also, but to a lesser degree, as early on travel downriver was thought to be dangerous, not only because of the conditions of the river itself, but also because of "the terrifying menace posed by the Indians" (Share 1982, 4). As we will see, however, the Ohio River would prove to be the major factor in Louisville's success.

Kentucky became a state in 1792, which "started a fresh influx of settlers into the territory and both the Wilderness Road through the Gap and the broad waterway of the Ohio were thronged with hordes of homesteaders" (McMeekin 1946, 32). Additionally, from the South, Louisville was the first port encountered upriver from New Orleans, thus serving as a port of entry for foreign goods (Share 1982).

After the Civil War, Pittsburgh began shipping more coal downriver, as Louisville began shipping lime upriver (Kleber 2001). Louisville became a regional distribution hub for flour, pork, tobacco, and other products headed south, and cotton, sugar, rice, and other products headed north (Share 1982). This position increased the contact between Northerners arriving via the Ohio and Southerners arriving via the Cumberland Gap. Though trade served as one of the main catalysts for contact, Northerners had long been migrating to Louisville (Turner 1911).

Thus, Louisville gained early success because of natural geographic advantages associated with the Ohio River, its proximity to established communities like Lexington and Cincinnati, and its location on the booming commerce highway. It further benefitted from the invention of the steam engine. By 1830, Louisville was the center of the steamboat industry, and river traffic increased (Share 1982). As Yater (2001, xvi) notes, "If the river made Louisville a town, the steamboat made Louisville a city." To this day, the *Belle of Louisville*, a steamboat built and put into service in 1914, is owned and operated by the city.

But soon the rail would take over as the preferred mode of transporting goods. Recognizing this trend and fearing a loss of power to upriver rival Cincinnati, Louisville sought a connection to its neighbor to the south, Nashville. "A railroad to the South would enable Louisville to break through its commercial isolation when the Ohio was impassable, to neutralize rival Nashville, and to gain the jump on Cincinnati in the quest for southern markets" (Share 1982, 36–37). This desire brought the creation of the L&N Railroad, which was completed to Nashville in 1859, establishing Louisville as "the Gateway to the South" (Share 1982, 37).

During the Civil War, Louisville's position on the Ohio River further added to the dichotomy experienced by residents. Louisville (and the rest of the state) was divided on the issue of slavery. As shown in figure 2.8, Kentucky was a disputed area. Despite having been claimed by the Confederate States of America, the state was never completely under its control.

This difficult position can be partially exemplified by a few facts. Kentucky was the only state to be officially represented at some point on both the Union and Confederate flags. Additionally, both the President of the Union, Abraham Lincoln, and the President of the Confederacy, Jefferson Davis, were Kentuckians (McMeekin 1946).

Because of these facts, some suggested that Kentucky should serve as mediator between the states, be impartial, and help restore peace. The state legislature declared neutrality in the war, which meant that the state chose not to align with the North or the South. When the Secretary of War requested four regiments of troops from Kentucky, the governor, Beriah Magoffin replied, "I say emphatically Kentucky will furnish no troops for the wicked purpose of subduing her sister Southern States" (McMeekin 1946, 128). Governor Magoffin declined a similar request from the Confederate forces.

Even though, as Yater (2001, xix) notes, "[a]s a border city in a slave state with commercial ties to the North as well as the South, Louisville attempted for a short while to adopt a neutral stance," both pro-Union and pro-Confederacy factions existed in Louisville (Beach 1995). Flags from both sides were flown on houses and businesses in the city. The two major newspapers in the city, the *Courier* and the *Journal,* differed in their

FIGURE 2.8
Confederate States of America

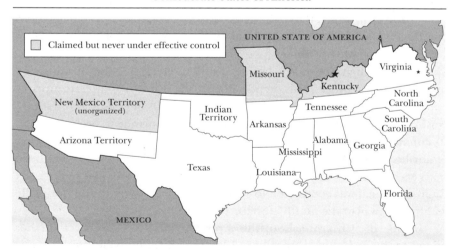

support: while the *Courier* supported the South, the *Journal* supported the North (McMeekin 1946).[4] Despite this seemingly divided stance, Union army recruits outnumbered Confederate ones three to one (Yater 2001).

This division, Kleber claims, came about because of the particular geography of the place, noting, "Located at the top of the South, it is separated by only a mile of water from the Midwest. Located in a slave state, it always faced south but it could never completely ignore the free territory at its back, although it did its best to do so" (2001, xi). This location also made it easy for pro-Union men in Louisville to simply cross into Northern territory, causing a breach of Kentucky's neutrality as Kentucky men joined the Union forces. Pro-Confederate men in the state also crossed borders to join the cause.

During the war, there was a federal ban on trade with the South, which caused great difficulty for Louisville's economy (Yater 2001). After the war, the editor at the *Louisville Daily Journal* suggested a need to resume trade with the South as soon as possible. To do so, a group of traveling salesmen known as drummers, many of whom were ex-Confederates, was established because "the community's merchants recognized that the city's 'southern-ness' could be an important psychological weapon in the battle with Cincinnati for the trade of the South" (Share 1982, 68). Thus, when dealing with Southern customers, Louisville's location within a former slave state was emphasized, and Cincinnati was positioned as a Yankee town (Share 1982; Yater 2001).

Louisville's rivalry with Cincinnati escalated when the Southern Commercial Convention was hosted in Cincinnati. As Henry Watterson, then-editor of the *Courier-Journal*, fumed:

to locate a Southern Convention there is doing violence to all outline maps of geography, common sense, history, and decency. There is nothing Southern in or about Cincinnati. In all the broad Southern land it is on record that Cincinnati is Southern, precisely as the carpet-baggers are Southern. She now reaches out her long, bony fingers [...] for Southern dollars and cents, just as she reached them out during the war for Southern cotton and Southern plantations. [quoted in Share 1982, 69]

In 1883, however, Louisville got its chance to shine as a beacon of commercialism in the South. Louisville hosted the Southern Exposition, a small, annual business fair, which "was meant to promote Louisville's developing industrial economy and its ability to serve as a transportation link between the North and the South" (Findling 2009, 52). The goal of this exposition was to strengthen Louisville's ties with traders in the North and South in order to continue in its position as a gateway city.

Thus, both in terms of its settlement history and its historic position of neutrality, Kentucky can historically be classified as belonging to both the North and the South. There is no better exemplar of this split position than Louisville. Yet, despite being both, there are ways in which Louisvillians position themselves more as being neither.

2.5. AT A CULTURAL BORDER

Despite the fact that claiming Louisville belonged to a former slave state had been of great importance for the economy at the time, today, for the most part, it seems that many Louisvillians do not emphasize their connections to the South. Louisville seems to stand apart from the rest of the state in many cultural respects.[5] Many depictions of the distinction place more emphasis on the rural-urban division within the state. Early on, the state had relatively few urban centers, of which Louisville was one. Share (1982, 20) notes, "By 1815 two societies had emerged in Kentucky, one rural and one urban, with distinct patterns of life, institutions, habits, and modes of thought." In describing these patterns of life, however, Share also notes that the cultural fare of Louisville varied, including activities like horse racing, dancing, and theatrical productions, which were typically associated with wealth and urbanity, as well as other less-refined activities like card playing, barbecues, and billiards, which seemed to be associated more with the nonwealthy. This establishes, in addition to the rural-urban division within the state, a class divide within the city. I would argue that the wealthy, urban practices listed above might also be associated with Northernness, while, to a lesser degree, the other practices could be described as Southern.

One way in which Louisville stands apart is in religion. Much like many Northern cities, and unlike the typically Protestant South, Louisville has a large population of Roman Catholics. As of 2000, the entire state boasted only 100.5 Roman Catholics per thousand people, though Jefferson County more than doubled that number, with 226.3 Roman Catholics per thousand. Catholics represent the largest religious group in Louisville, while Kentucky as a whole has a larger percentage of Southern Baptist adherents (Association of Religion Data Archive 2010). Thus, Louisville has been described as "one of the few heavily Catholic urban areas in the American South" (Kleber 2001, 768).

This, however, has not always been the case. In 1845, there was a large number of immigrants who arrived in Louisville from Ireland because of the potato famine and from Germany because of a failed revolution. These immigrants, largely Catholic, changed the predominantly Protestant face of the city. Unfortunately, the political climate, which saw the rise of the Know-Nothings in the 1850s, led to violence against Louisville's Catholics, culminating in what has been called "Bloody Monday," a riot that killed at least 22 (Yater 2001, xviii).

The Catholic Church in Louisville has a rich and important history in terms of American Catholicism. While the first church established in Louisville was Episcopalian, the Catholics were not far behind. The Diocese of Baltimore was the first and only Catholic diocese in the United States until Pope Pius VII added Bardstown, Kentucky, as a diocese, spanning a large portion of the middle of the country. Eventually the See, or administrative center, of that diocese was transferred to Louisville (McMeekin 1946).

Another way in which Louisville is different from the rest of the state can be seen in its political stance. More liberals can be found in Louisville, whereas the rest of the state tends to be more conservative. In the 2004 presidential election, for instance, only 48.78% of ballots cast in Jefferson County went to Bush-Cheney, whereas they pulled 59.55% of the ballots cast in the rest of the state. Additionally, in a 2004 Senate race, Louisville chose democratic candidate Daniel Mongiardo by nearly 2:1 (59.58%), but Jim Bunning, the republican candidate, won the state with 50.66% of the vote (Kentucky State Board of Elections 2004). Furthermore, in local politics, Republican candidates rarely ever won a Louisville mayoral contest during the twentieth century. Kleber notes (2001, 756),

The Kentucky Republican Party and its arm in Louisville and Jefferson County have led parallel lives. They each historically do well in presidential and congressional elections, but Democrats rule when voters choose state and local officials. It is a phenomenon manifested by registration figures in Jefferson County, where Democrats outregister Republicans by about two to one.

History, again, plays a role in how this division came about. Bolstered by the influx of Irish and Germans immigrants in the mid-1800s, the number of Democrats rose in opposition to the Know-Nothings party, which tended toward anti-Catholic violence, as evidenced by the events of "Bloody Monday" (Kleber 2001).

Despite these differences, Louisville represents Kentucky on the national and international level, especially during events like the Kentucky Derby, when the sports world focuses on the city and its residents. In an editorial in the *Courier-Journal* (2009), one writer explains, "On this day, more than any other, the split personality of our border city tends toward the southern." These types of descriptions associate this event with an expression of Southernness, suggesting that the popular media see Louisville as a representative Southern city.

2.6. AT A PERCEPTUAL BORDER

Beyond these geopolitical, sociohistorical facts, it is also important to note how previous studies in folk dialectology add to our understanding of Louisville as being located at a border. In his "Five Visions of America," Preston (1989) showed that, in drawing maps of regional variation, respondents from southern Indiana, New York City, and western New York place the boundary of the South and the Midwest or North along the Ohio River. The map in figure 2.9 (Preston 1989, 114), for example, shows the composite vision of American dialects as described by people from New York City. Again, as with others maps we have seen in this chapter, the Ohio River forms the northern border of the Southern dialect region according to New Yorkers.

Additionally, respondents from Hawaii and Michigan do not include Louisville in either of these designations, leaving the city without a region. The map in figure 2.10 (Preston 1989, 116) is a composite of maps rep-

FIGURE 2.9

Composite Map of Dialect Regions from New York City Respondents
(Preston 1989, 114)

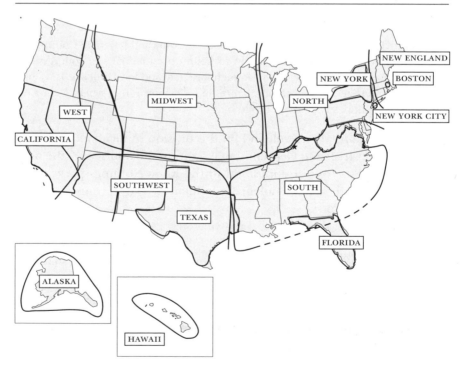

resenting the mental maps drawn by Michigan respondents. Here, Louisville and other parts of Kentucky and southern Indiana are left without a regional category. The act of leaving Louisville uncategorized suggests that Michiganders are either completely unfamiliar with the variety spoken there, or, perhaps more likely, they are confused by the perceived mixture of linguistic cultures in the area.

Such maps are created, as will be shown in later chapters, by combining the hand-drawn maps created by individuals from a place. For example, the map in figure 2.11, from Preston (1989, 27), shows the dialect areas drawn by a college student from Hawaii. This fairly detailed map shows that this respondent also sees the Ohio River as playing a role in dialect differentiation. In this case, Kentucky is represented as one of the northernmost locations in the region where "Southern Twang" is spoken.

Of particular interest in terms of the border perceptions is what Preston (1989, 69) found with his southern Indiana respondents, as they live just across the river from Louisville. He found that when they "draw bound-

FIGURE 2.10
Composite Map of Dialect Regions from Michigan Respondents
(Preston 1989, 116)

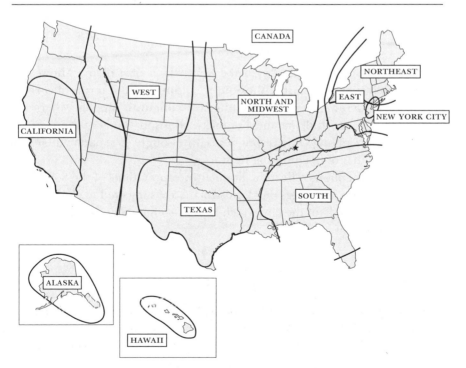

FIGURE 2.11

Individual Map of Dialect Regions from a Hawaiian Respondent
(Preston 1989, 27)

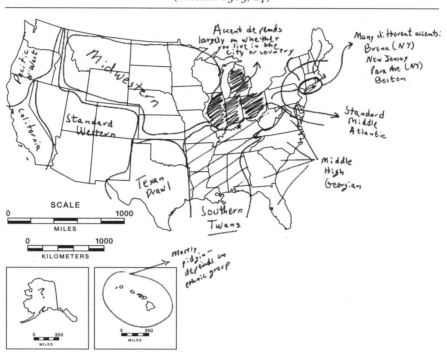

aries around speech areas they make Kentucky a part of the Midwest as often as they make it a part of the South," adding that, in terms of correctness ratings, another key component of folk linguistic studies, "there is a great gulf between Indiana and Kentucky." Benson (2003) found similar differentiation among Ohio respondents, who sought to separate their own speech from that of neighboring Kentucky.

These perceptions reflect the popular interpretations of the South and its boundary, and it suggests that Louisvillians are subjected to classification from people outside of the city, which likely also has some bearing on how they classify themselves.

2.7. DISCUSSION

One final way we might consider Louisville as being located at the border is agriculturally. If we consider where the quintessential Midwestern crop, corn, is grown, we find that very little corn is produced in Kentucky as a whole, let alone in a large metropolitan area like Louisville (figure 2.12). But, if we examine where kudzu, an invasive ivy-like plant found across the South, grows we'll also see no evidence of it near Louisville (figure 2.13). Thus, with no corn and no kudzu, and all of the other factors presented above, how can one understand Louisville's regional location?

On an insert, presumably from the cover, in Isabel McLennan McMeekin's (1946) discussion about Louisville as a gateway city, it claims,

This is the story of a city which has always been called the gateway from the North to the South, where the best Southern traditions of gracious living are combined with vigorous northern qualities of thriving business and industrial growth.

Simply put, Louisville has a history of being located between North and South, and in this chapter, I have shown that Louisville is, in fact, located at many types of borders, going beyond gracious living and thriving business to look at the facts of geography and history, among others, in portraying the dichotomous nature of this great city. These borders are more than lines on a map; these borders influence not only how Louisvillians see themselves in terms of regionality, but also how Louisvillians are seen by others.

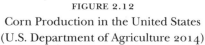

FIGURE 2.12
Corn Production in the United States
(U.S. Department of Agriculture 2014)

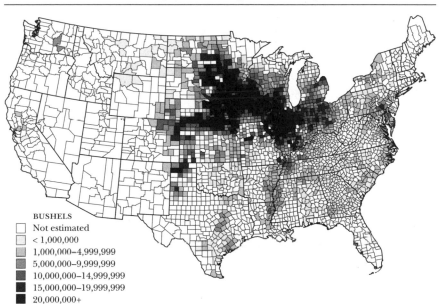

BUSHELS
☐ Not estimated
☐ < 1,000,000
▨ 1,000,000–4,999,999
▨ 5,000,000–9,999,999
■ 10,000,000–14,999,999
■ 15,000,000–19,999,999
■ 20,000,000+

FIGURE 2.13

Propagation of Kudzu in the Southern United States

(Wolfram 2003, 124)

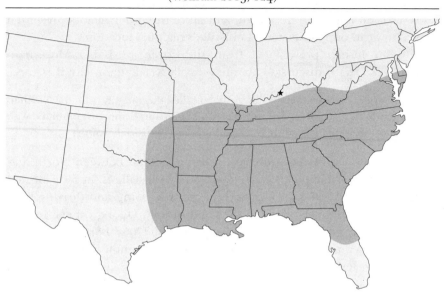

3. INSIDER PERCEPTIONS
OF THE DIALECT LANDSCAPE

As THE PREVIOUS CHAPTER has shown, Louisville is situated in the dialect landscape of the United States at a particularly interesting crossroads. This location between Southern and Midwestern cultural regions and between Southern and Midland dialects, I argue, impacts how Louisvillians discuss language and linguistic variation in their country.

In this chapter, I explore how Louisvillians understand the dialect landscape of the United States as a whole, their larger regional area, and the state of Kentucky specifically. Drawing on many types of data and on insights in the field of perceptual dialectology, specifically following the work of Preston (Preston 1989, 1999; Long and Preston 2002), this chapter details the folk perceptions about dialectal variation held by people in Louisville, thus establishing the on-the-ground categories used by Louisvillians to construct their image of national, regional, and statewide linguistic variation. In so doing, it showcases the groups with which Louisvillians identify and those from whom they may wish to dissociate, a topic that is further explored in chapter 4.

3.1. CORRECTNESS AND PLEASANTNESS RATINGS

Aside from mental mapping, one of the most common practices of perceptual dialectologists working within the modern tradition is to ask nonlinguists to rate individual states and cities in terms of how correct or pleasant its linguistic variety is perceived to be. In this section, I examine how Louisvillians completed this task in order to present the broadest way in which Louisvillians perceive linguistic variation in the country.

The data for this section come from an online survey of 68 Kentuckians, 35 of whom were from Louisville, in which participants were asked to rate each of the 50 states, New York City, and Washington, D.C., in terms of degree of difference (covered in chapter 4), correctness, and pleasantness. As discussed in chapter 1, for correctness and pleasantness ratings, participants were given a 10-point scale on which a lower score indicated a lower level of correctness or pleasantness.

The image in figure 3.1 is a choropleth map representing the average ratings given to each state and the two cities by Louisvillians for level of cor-

43

FIGURE 3.1
Louisvillians' Correctness Ratings

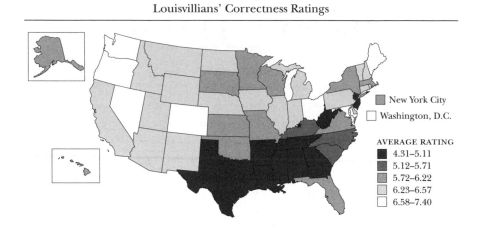

rectness. The darkest colored states represent those seen as least correct; thus, it appears that Louisvillians believe most of the Southern states, West Virginia, and New Jersey to be in this lowest range, with Alabama receiving the lowest average rating of 4.31. Maine, Maryland, Ohio, Colorado, Nevada, and those states in the Pacific Northwest, as well as Washington, D.C., are perceived to be most correct, with Washington, D.C., receiving the highest average rating of 7.40.

Figure 3.2 shows the average ratings given by Louisvillians to individual states and cities for level of pleasantness. New Jersey and Tennessee are represented in the darkest color, indicating that they were rated least pleasant, with New Jersey receiving the lowest average rating of 4.34. Hawaii, Califor-

FIGURE 3.2
Louisvillians' Pleasantness Ratings

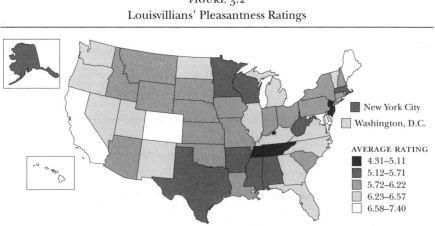

nia, Colorado, Maryland, and Maine are considered to be most pleasant, with Hawaii receiving the highest average rating of 6.71.

Together these maps reveal some interesting tendencies. For example, Louisvillians think rather highly of the speech in Maine, Maryland, and Colorado, such that these states received the highest average ratings in terms of both correctness and pleasantness. They also think very little of Tennessee and New Jersey, which were both rated very low on both dimensions. The correctness ratings match well with many other perceptual dialectology studies that categorize the Southern states as being less correct, but those same studies typically show that participants balance this distaste for Southern speech by rating it highly in pleasantness, likely as a result of the "stupid but friendly" stereotype of Southerners (e.g., Hartley 1999; Niedzielski and Preston 2000). While Florida, Georgia, North Carolina, and Virginia are rated with Kentucky in the range just below the most pleasant range, the rest of the South, most notably Tennessee, are rated rather poorly in this dimension.

To explore further how these individual state numbers relate to larger regional understandings of variation, I have combined the states into regions, based on Fridland and Bartlett's (2006) divisions seen in figure 3.3, and calculated regional means for correctness and pleasantness.[1] These ratings can be found in table 3.1.

FIGURE 3.3
Regional Divisions, from Fridland and Bartlett (2006, 364)

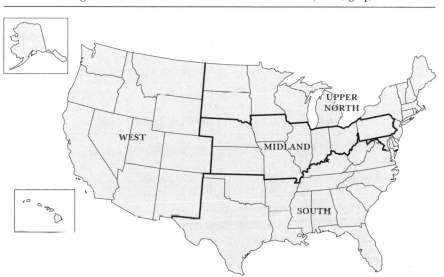

TABLE 3.1

Average Ratings and Ranking for Correctness and Pleasantness by Region

	Correctness		Pleasantness	
	Mean Rating	Rank	Mean Rating	Rank
South	5.75	5	6.04	5
Upper North	6.64	4	6.10	4
Midland	6.80	2	6.20	3
West	6.91	1	6.49	1
Other	6.74	3	6.36	2

From these averages, we see that the South as a whole is rated lowest in both correctness and pleasantness, while the West is rated highest in these two dimensions. The notion of the pleasant West is also not unheard of, as Fridland and Bartlett's (2006) Memphis, Tennessee, participants tended to categorize the West in this way, as did their Reno, Nevada, participants. The difference between the means here, however, shows that Louisvillians typically gave responses in the middle of the range for all states, such that the difference between the least and most correct regions is only slightly higher than one point, and the difference in level of pleasantness is at less than half a point. In fact, as the information in table 3.2 shows, a one-way analysis of variance (ANOVA) calculated on participants' ratings of correctness and pleasantness reveal that the differences are not significant at $p < .05$, $F(4,160) = 1.62$, $p = 0.17$ for correctness and $F(4,161) = 0.36$, $p = 0.84$ for pleasantness.

This lack of significance (and the fact that the means were so close together) may also be indicative of Louisville's border nature. While it is possible that half of the participants rated the states at one end of the rating scale while the other half rated them at the other end (not supported by

TABLE 3.2

ANOVA Results for Level of Correctness and Pleasantness

Source of Variation	Sum of Squares	df	Mean Square	F	p-Value
Correctness					
Between groups	29.16671	4	7.291678	1.622172	.171197
Within groups	719.2014	160	4.495009		
TOTAL	748.3682	164			
Pleasant					
Between groups	4.761897	4	1.190474	0.359577	.837077
Within groups	533.0324	161	3.3176		
TOTAL	537.7943	165			

the individual ratings), in actuality, Louisvillians gave most states an average rating such that no particular state was rated very high or very low on the scales. Perhaps this is a result of the task itself, such that individuals with no justification for rating a certain state high or low on the scale chose to assign it a median score; the result, however, is that Louisvillians appear to regard no state and no region as particularly correct or pleasant. Their view of the larger dialect landscape in the United States is that of equality—all varieties are equally correct and incorrect, equally pleasant and unpleasant. But when we examine how they responded to the mental map drawing task, it is clear that all varieties are not created equal in the eyes of Louisvillians.

3.2. REGIONAL DIALECT LANDSCAPE

Having examined how Louisvillians rate all the states, we can zoom in to a smaller region to see how Louisvillians perceive variation in their regional dialect landscape. In this section, I present some of the individual mental maps drawn by the 23 participants from Louisville when asked to draw dialect boundaries on a map of a small region of the United States with Kentucky at its center (see figure 1.6). I present the most and least detailed maps, as well as a map that showcases some of the common practices of participants, thus providing a picture of the tendencies found among Louisvillians in this map drawing task.

These tendencies are made more concrete through the presentation of composite maps, a single map that combines all regions drawn on individual mental maps. These maps, created through the use of ArcGIS (cf. Montgomery and Stoeckle 2013), a geographic information systems tool, provide an overall picture of how Louisvillians see regional variation in this smaller segment of the United States.[2] Additionally, I examine the results of a language attitudes survey that accompanied this regional map drawing task to highlight the perceptions Louisvillians have of the regions they delimit with respect to degree of difference (discussed in chapter 4), correctness, pleasantness, standardness, formality, beauty, and level of education.

Figure 3.4 is the least detailed map completed by a participant using the larger regional map. This map, which features only one region labeled "Southern Twang," was created by a 19-year-old white male who was born and raised in Louisville. His Southern region, which was by far larger than any other Southern region drawn by participants in this study, encompasses mostly noncoastal Southern areas, as has often not been the case in other perceptual dialectology studies (Preston 1989, 30; see figure 1.8). Addition-

FIGURE 3.4
Least Detailed Dialect Map of Larger Region,
Drawn by a 19-Year-Old White Male Louisvillian

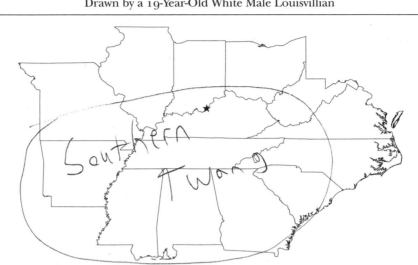

ally, his Southern region not only encompasses Louisville, but also areas across the Ohio River in southern Illinois, Indiana, and Ohio, thus including the entire state of Kentucky in the Southern region, which indicates that this participant fails to see the Ohio River as any sort of demarcation of the Southern region, unlike many other characterizations of the river as such.

Figure 3.5 is the most detailed map completed by a participant using the larger regional map. This map, which features 16 different regions and notably divides Louisville itself into three distinct regions, was created by a 31-year-old white male who was born in Louisville and spent a short period of time elsewhere for college.[3] His division of the dialect landscape is even more complex than that typically created by linguists. In addition to his meticulous attention to Kentucky and Louisville, this participant indicates some variation in Appalachian varieties, as evidenced by separate regions in eastern Kentucky and western North Carolina. Unlike the participant who drew the map in figure 3.4, this participant's Southern region is confined to what is typically described as the Deep South (Mississippi, Alabama, and Georgia) and does not adjoin the region labeled "Bland Midwest Normalcy" at the Ohio River, thus relegating Louisville as well as the southern portions of Illinois, Indiana, and Ohio as regional no-man's-lands.

Another rather detailed map can be found in figure 3.6. This participant, a 40-year-old white female who claimed to have lived only six months outside of Louisville, identified 11 different regions, including a separate

FIGURE 3.5
Most Detailed Dialect Map of Larger Region,
Drawn by a 31-Year-Old White Male Louisvillian

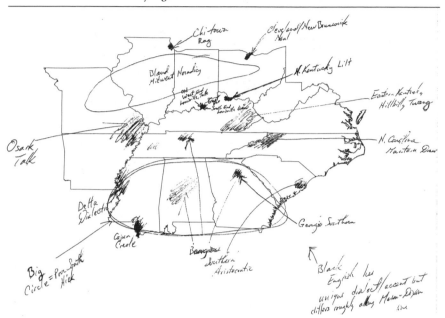

"Southern Urban" region that encompasses both Louisville and Lexington. This connection between Louisville and Lexington was found in a few maps and is not unexpected. As the two largest cities in the state, both home to major state universities and both with relatively recent mergers of their city and county governments, these similar cities stand out as different from the rest of the mostly rural state (see Cramer 2016).

The divisions made in this map represent most of the more commonly encircled areas found in this study and can be seen as a typical Louisvillian's representation of the larger regional dialect landscape. Some of these areas, like this participant's Chicago accent region, appeared on many participant maps, yet it does not match any of the categories in Preston's (1989) template. Additionally, this participant's "Coal E. Ky accent Mt. Folk" region roughly lines up with an Appalachian region, which was the second most frequently delimited region in this study after Southern. Therefore, to address the analytical difficulty that arises from the free choice of labels given in such a task, geography, frequency, and Preston's template were used to guide the selection of regions included in the composite maps, as described in chapter 1.[4]

The most commonly delimited areas in this data set were Appalachia, Cajun/Creole, Chicago, Georgia, Kentucky, Louisville/Lexington, Mid-

FIGURE 3.6

Dialect Regions Drawn by a 40-Year-Old White Female Louisvillian

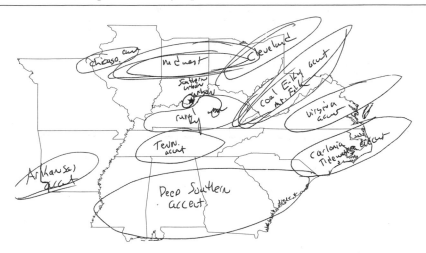

Atlantic, Midwest, Northern, Southern, and Tennessee. These 11 overarching categories serve as the regional delimiters in the composite map. In what follows, I present and discuss eight of these regions (the remaining three will be discussed in the chapter 4) through the use of heat maps.[5]

I begin by discussing the Appalachia region. In figure 3.7, we see that the core of this region is situated rather accurately in terms of the geographic space of the Appalachian Mountains, which seemed to be the motivation for participants who selected this region. The darkest shading is in eastern Kentucky, an area that Louisvillians have likely come to know as quite different from their own, whether through actually visiting the area, as many participants indicated, or simply through stereotypes, also commonly suggested by participants. One participant, however, appears to link his variety of speech in Louisville to the speech of Appalachia.

Despite the fact that Louisiana does not appear on this map, some Louisvillians had a desire to represent a Cajun/Creole dialect in this landscape, as evidenced by figure 3.8. Here, the Mississippi and Alabama coastlines represent the core of this area. Again, either through travel or stereotypes, it appears that Louisvillians find this region to be distinct enough to deserve indication. This is the only label that draws on a possible ethnic tie and is the only dialect where a mixture of languages was represented as the key element (hence, the overarching label Cajun/Creole). This region is considerably smaller than other regions, and it was represented on only four participants' maps.

FIGURE 3.7
Composite of the Appalachia Dialect Region, Drawn by 14 Louisvillians

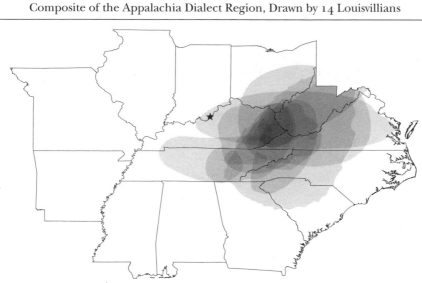

FIGURE 3.8
Composite of the Cajun/Creole Dialect Region, Drawn by 4 Louisvillians

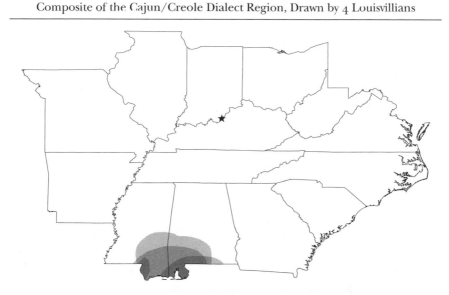

Figure 3.9 is the composite map of the Chicago region. The core of this region fairly accurately centers on the area of northeastern Illinois on Lake Michigan where Chicago is situated. Some participants took some liberties with their definition of Chicago by not even encompassing the

FIGURE 3.9
Composite of the Chicago Dialect Region, Drawn by 7 Louisvillians

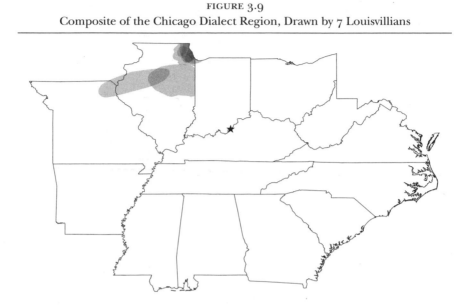

city itself. While it is perhaps likely that these participants omitted the city itself and selected these other areas in Illinois and even Missouri because of geographic incompetence, it is also possible that they were attempting to suggest that the speech of Chicago is broader than the city limits. Like the Cajun/Creole region, this area is rather small. Yet the number of respondents who acknowledged Chicago as a distinct dialect was twice that of the Cajun/Creole number. In their descriptions of the Chicago dialect, participants focused on the metropolitan or urban nature of the city. Yet again, however, stereotypes seem to play a large role in the delimitation of a Chicago region, as one participant mentioned "Bill Swerski's Superfans," a popular recurring sketch from *Saturday Night Live* in the 1990s, indicating that even if Louisvillians do not have much physical connection to an area, they can recognize that a variety exists through the expression of stereotypes.

Moving beyond regional, ethnic, and city labels, figure 3.10 represents a particular state, Georgia, as a distinct dialect for Louisvillians. The core of this dialect is centered in the state and seems to be disconnected from Atlanta, the major urban center in the state, which is located to the northwest of the core. This disconnect is further indicated in the participants' discussion of their labels, where they focus on the rural nature of the state.

Louisvillians also recognized Tennessee as a distinct region, which can be seen in figure 3.11. The core of this region is in central Tennessee, with

FIGURE 3.10
Composite of the Georgia Dialect Region, Drawn by 4 Louisvillians

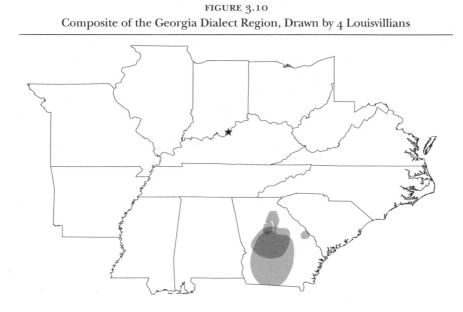

FIGURE 3.11
Composite of the Tennessee Dialect Region, Drawn by 5 Louisvillians

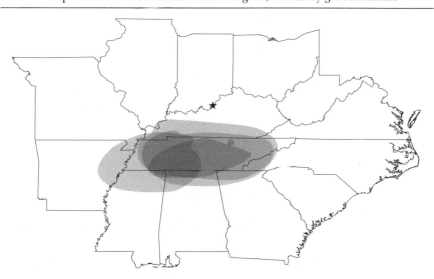

a small portion of northern Alabama and Mississippi also included in the core. Unlike Georgia, the whole of Tennessee, with the exception of the northeast corner, is considered under this label. Additionally, parts of Kentucky, mostly along the state line, and other states are subsumed under this Tennessee dialect. Quite like what we will see with Kentucky, Louisvillians present Tennessee in a rather negative light. This suggests a need among Louisvillians to distinguish their own dialect from a dialect they perceive to be nonstandard, uneducated, and, in the words of one participant, "nasally—sometimes irritating if high pitched."

Another state Louisvillians defined was Kentucky, as represented in figure 3.12. The core of this region seems to be in central Kentucky, perhaps near or connected to Lexington. For at least two of the six participants, this definition of Kentucky includes Louisville, while the others chose to exclude it. Like Tennessee, the majority of the state is included under this label, with the exception of some small areas in eastern, western, and northern Kentucky left undefined here.

Aside from being the core of Kentucky, Lexington, along with Louisville, was represented on six maps as a distinct speech area, as seen in figure 3.13. One participant even connected Columbus, Ohio as the same as the dialect spoken in these two Kentucky cities. Rather impressively, the participants in Louisville designated the core of this Louisville-dominant variety in the geographic space of Louisville, as indicated by the star. The two participants who included Lexington did not agree on its geographic location. This region is even smaller than the Chicago region, suggesting that Louisvillians do not really believe their own dialect spreads very far from the city.

FIGURE 3.12
Composite of the Kentucky Dialect Region, Drawn by 6 Louisvillians

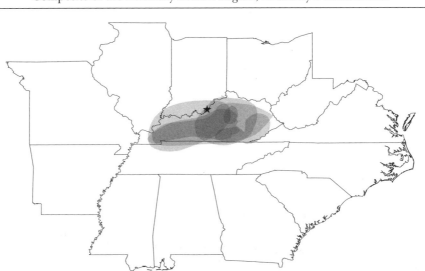

FIGURE 3.13

Composite of the Louisville/Lexington Dialect Region, Drawn by 8 Louisvillians

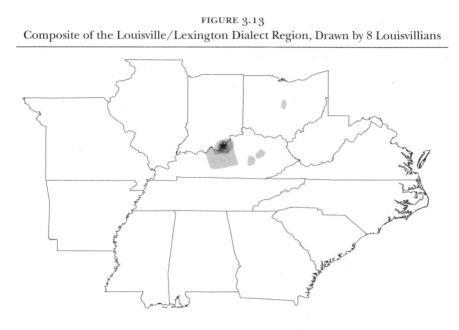

A regional distinction can be found in figure 3.14, where we see how Louisvillians define the Mid-Atlantic region on the East Coast. The core of this region is in central Virginia, with a large group suggesting a connection both to the coast and to the greater Washington, D.C., area. This was one of

FIGURE 3.14

Composite of the Mid-Atlantic Dialect Region, Drawn by 7 Louisvillians

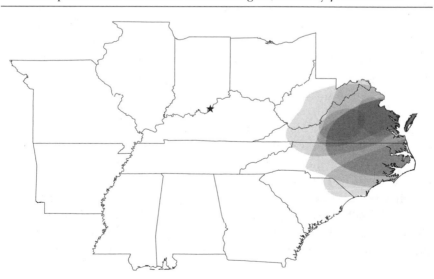

the most diverse regions defined by Louisvillians, in that their representations of the region varied from emphasis on the mountain portions of these states, even though they delimited regions with coastlines, to emphasis on the proper, upper-crust way of speaking perceived there. It seems that even though seven participants delineated this region, Louisvillians as a whole are a little confused about the language spoken there. This confusion likely arises either from differences in experiences with people in the region or from geographic incompetence. Again, it appears that Louisvillians are certain that a variety exists there, even if they cannot agree on the type, nature, and location of it.

The individual composite maps for the Midwest, Southern, and Northern regions will be discussed in chapter 4. But this examination of several heat maps makes it clear that, in attempting to produce an overall regional picture of variation, Preston (1989, 28) was correct when he claimed that "neither the minimal boundaries [...] nor the maximal ones [...] will do as a generalization" of the perceptions speakers have about varieties of American English. If we included all of the individually drawn regions in one map, there would be significant overlap, such that the composite would be basically useless. If we included only the darkest shaded areas from those regions, the areas that everyone agreed upon, the shared understanding of Louisvillians of the dialect landscape would consist only of small patches in a few places. To address this issue, I present in figure 3.15 the composite map of the regions in which the areas shaded were agreed upon by 50% of participants who included the region.

This map is rather complex. For instance, both the Mid-Atlantic and Midwest regions consist of two large disconnected pieces. The Southern region subsumes both the Cajun/Creole and the Georgia regions, the second of which is but two very small points on the map. Part of the Midwest region overlaps with the Northern region, which is almost completely confined to Ohio. Chicago, which appears as two small regions, stands alone as separate from the Midwest region, which is also the way in which Louisvillians described it. The Tennessee and Kentucky regions fill in a great majority of their state space, with only a small amount of overlap in western Kentucky. Tennessee also overlaps slightly with the Southern region. The Appalachia region here is much more condensed, and the fact that it is centered in Eastern Kentucky shows that this representation closely matches the part of Appalachia that the participants were describing in their surveys. There is also some overlap between the Kentucky and Appalachia regions and between the Kentucky and Louisville/Lexington regions, the latter of which is now trimmed down to include only Louisville.

FIGURE 3.15
Overall Composite Map of Louisvillians' Responses with 50% Agreement

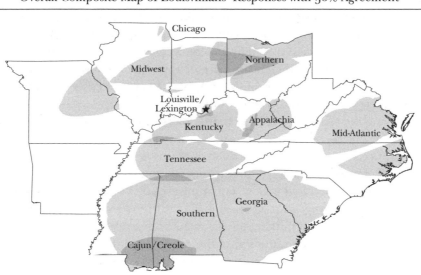

But the picture is not complete without considering, in addition to this broad understanding of the dialect landscape of this region of the United States, the attitudes held by participants about these varieties. In the language attitudes survey that accompanied the map drawing task, participants were asked to list each of the labels they employed on the hand-drawn map on a separate page of the survey and were asked to answer a set of ten questions about that variety, including seven questions about social characteristics on a four-point scale and three open-ended questions. The questions used in this study can be found in the appendix.

The analysis of language attitudes involves the post hoc statistical test known as the Tukey HSD (Honestly Significant Difference) test. A post hoc analysis is necessary, as the categories used by participants were not determined before the experiment. This test is a variation of the t distribution, using instead the studentized range distribution q. This method is used to compare all pairs of means of every treatment and is used instead of multiple standard t-tests to reduce the likelihood of type I errors. This method was also selected because it can handle unequal sample sizes, as found in my data. Like a t-test, a critical value must be determined in order to decide whether the result is significant. A result is significant if the q-value calculated is larger than the q critical value determined in a distribution table.[6]

For each of the social factors, I determined the number of responses and the mean values of the responses for each of the 11 overarching categories. I then ranked the mean values for each region over the entire category. For instance, in terms of correctness, the Appalachia region, with a mean score of 3.00, had the highest mean value, giving it a rank of 11, while the Chicago region, with a mean score of 1.57, had the lowest mean value, giving it a rank of 1. That means that Appalachia is viewed as rather low on the correctness scale and Chicago rather high.

Using the ranking system, I created pairs of regions under each social category. The first pair was always the lowest and highest ranking means in the group. After performing the analysis of this pair, the next pair consisted in the region with the lowest ranking mean and the second highest ranking mean. The analysis continues as such until a result is returned that is not significant. The pairings start again, this time with the second lowest ranking mean and the highest ranking mean, again until a result is returned that is not significant. This continues until the comparison of any first region and the highest ranked region returns a result that is not significant.[7]

Here, I present the findings of the analysis, looking at each social characteristic individually. Each discussion includes two tables: one features an alphabetical list of the regions and their respective number of responses, means, and ranking, and the other lists the individual pairings, with their respective number of responses, means, and ranking, as well as the computed q-value, the q critical value, and the decision on significance (in which TRUE means that the result was significant).

Table 3.3 lists the information about how Louisvillians perceive the level of correctness among the 11 regions they have defined. Table 3.4

TABLE 3.3
Summary of Level of Correctness

	n	Mean Rating	Rank
Appalachia	14	3.00	11
Cajun/Creole	4	2.75	9
Chicago	7	1.57	1
Georgia	4	2.75	9
Kentucky	6	2.50	7
Louisville/Lexington	8	1.88	4
Mid-Atlantic	7	2.29	6
Midwest	7	1.57	1
Northern	8	1.75	3
Southern	21	2.19	5
Tennessee	5	2.60	8

features the 12 different pairings involved in the analysis of level of correctness. Looking at the means and rankings for the level of correctness, Louisvillians perceive an Appalachia dialect to be the least correct way of speaking and a Chicago or Midwest dialect (tied) as the most correct way of speaking. These results indicate that Louisvillians believe the Appalachian dialect to be statistically significantly less correct than the Chicago, Midwest, Northern, Louisville/Lexington, and Southern dialects. There were no other statistically significant differences in level of correctness.

The rankings also provide interesting information. For instance, Chicago, the Midwest, and the North are all categorized rather high on the correctness scale, while Appalachia, Cajun/Creole, Georgia, and Tennes-

TABLE 3.4
Analysis of Pairings for Level of Correctness

	n	Mean Rating	Rank	q	q-Critical	Significant?
Appalachia	14	3.00	11	6.446270	4.65	TRUE
Chicago	7	1.57	1			
Appalachia	14	3.00	11	6.446270	4.65	TRUE
Midwest	7	1.57	1			
Appalachia	14	3.00	11	5.891296	4.65	TRUE
Northern	8	1.75	3			
Appalachia	14	3.00	11	5.302166	4.65	TRUE
Louisville/Lexington	8	1.88	4			
Appalachia	14	3.00	11	4.900861	4.65	TRUE
Southern	21	2.19	5			
Appalachia	14	3.00	11	3.223135	4.65	FALSE
Mid-Atlantic	7	2.29	6			
Cajun/Creole	4	2.75	9	3.927731	4.65	FALSE
Chicago	7	1.57	1			
Cajun/Creole	4	2.75	9	3.927731	4.65	FALSE
Midwest	7	1.57	1			
Georgia	4	2.75	9	3.927731	4.65	FALSE
Chicago	7	1.57	1			
Georgia	4	2.75	9	3.927731	4.65	FALSE
Midwest	7	1.57	1			
Tennessee	5	2.60	8	3.669281	4.65	FALSE
Chicago	7	1.57	1			
Tennessee	5	2.60	8	3.669281	4.65	FALSE
Midwest	7	1.57	1			

see are rated rather low. These results mirror many folk linguistic studies, as well as the results of the correctness survey discussed in the previous section, which find Southern varieties to be typically rated as less correct. What is interesting, however, is that the overarching category Southern itself is not so poorly rated; in fact, it rates in the top 50% of the categories here. Kentucky does not rate in the top 50%, falling just below the Mid-Atlantic dialect.

Table 3.5 presents how Louisvillians perceive the level of pleasantness among these regions. The ratings resulted in four pairings in the analysis of significance for level of pleasantness, as presented in table 3.6. From these tables we can see that Louisvillians perceive a Tennessee dialect to be the least pleasant dialect and the more general Southern dialect as the most pleasant. These results indicate, however, that the only statistically signifi-

TABLE 3.5
Summary of Level of Pleasantness

	n	Mean Rating	Rank
Appalachia	14	2.14	5
Cajun/Creole	4	2.25	8
Chicago	7	2.00	4
Georgia	4	2.50	10
Kentucky	6	2.17	7
Louisville/Lexington	8	1.75	2
Mid-Atlantic	7	2.14	5
Midwest	7	1.86	3
Northern	8	2.25	8
Southern	21	1.62	1
Tennessee	5	2.80	11

TABLE 3.6
Analysis of Pairings for Level of Pleasantness

	n	Mean Rating	Rank	q	q-Critical	Significant?
Tennessee	5	2.80	11	4.821525	4.65	TRUE
Southern	21	1.62	1			
Tennessee	5	2.80	11	3.741896	4.65	FALSE
Louisville/Lexington	8	1.75	2			
Georgia	4	2.50	10	3.280697	4.65	FALSE
Southern	21	1.62	1			
Northern	8	2.25	10	3.085292	4.65	FALSE
Southern	21	1.62	1			

cant difference in pleasantness perceived by Louisvillians is between these two dialects. There were no other statistically significant results.

We can turn to the rankings again to glean some additional results. The most interesting fact is the rather low ratings for Cajun/Creole, Georgia, and Tennessee, despite the very high rating for Southern. The high rating in pleasantness for Southern speech is not unexpected, as many folk linguistic studies have highlighted the common understanding of the American South as typically pleasant but not correct. For example, Fridland and Bartlett (2006) found that people from Memphis, Tennessee, like many Southerners, found their region to be generally pleasant but relatively incorrect when compared to the North. Often in these studies, however, the geographic areas delimited by Cajun/Creole, Georgia, and Tennessee are often subsumed under the Southern category. This fact, in addition to the fact that Louisvillians included these regions on their maps at all, suggests that these regions are distinct areas for Louisvillians and that they are not held in very high regard.

Information about how Louisvillians perceive level of standardness for these regions can be found in table 3.7. The analysis of significance in table 3.8 features nine different pairings involved in the analysis of level of standardness. The results of the statistical test reveal that, for level of standardness, Louisvillians perceive a Cajun/Creole dialect to be the least standard dialect and the Louisville/Lexington dialect as the most standard. Louisvillians believe the Cajun/Creole and Appalachia dialects to be statistically significantly less standard than the Louisville/Lexington dialect. Also, the Appalachian dialect was rated as statistically significantly less standard than

TABLE 3.7
Summary of Level of Standardness

	n	Mean Rating	Rank
Appalachia	14	2.93	10
Cajun/Creole	4	3.00	11
Chicago	7	1.86	2
Georgia	4	2.75	9
Kentucky	6	2.33	5
Louisville/Lexington	8	1.75	1
Mid-Atlantic	7	2.43	7
Midwest	7	1.86	2
Northern	8	2.13	4
Southern	21	2.48	8
Tennessee	5	2.40	6

TABLE 3.8
Analysis of Pairings for Level of Standardness

	n	Mean Rating	Rank	q	q-Critical	Significant?
Cajun/Creole	4	3.00	11	4.773808	4.65	TRUE
Louisville/Lexington	8	1.75	1			
Cajun/Creole	4	3.00	11	4.264275	4.65	FALSE
Chicago	7	1.86	2			
Cajun/Creole	4	3.00	11	4.264275	4.65	FALSE
Midwest	7	1.86	2			
Appalachia	14	2.93	10	6.219051	4.65	TRUE
Louisville/Lexington	8	1.75	1			
Appalachia	14	2.93	10	5.412989	4.65	TRUE
Chicago	7	1.86	2			
Appalachia	14	2.93	10	5.412989	4.65	TRUE
Midwest	7	1.86	2			
Appalachia	14	2.93	10	4.240262	4.65	FALSE
Northern	8	2.13	4			
Georgia	4	2.75	9	3.819046	4.65	FALSE
Louisville/Lexington	8	1.75	1			
Southern	21	2.48	8	4.087679	4.65	FALSE
Louisville/Lexington	8	1.75	1			

the Chicago and Midwest dialects. There were no other statistically significant results.

The rankings indicate that, like with level of correctness, Louisvillians believe many of the dialects in the Southern United States to be less standard than the Chicago, Midwest, and Northern dialects. However, unlike with the level of correctness, the Southern dialect itself also receives a poor rating in terms of standardness. This fact suggests that standardness must mean something different to Louisvillians than correctness. This is further evidenced by the information provided in the open-ended questions, where many people seem to associate these non-Southern varieties with news anchors, and the news industry is often associated with a variety commonly known as Standard American English.

Means and rankings calculated for level of formality among these regions are listed in table 3.9. Given these ratings, the analysis of significance for level of formality can be seen in table 3.10, which features 12 different pairings. In this category, Louisvillians perceive a Kentucky dialect to be the least formal dialect and the Louisville/Lexington dialect as the most formal. These results indicate that Louisvillians believe the Kentucky and

TABLE 3.9
Summary of Level of Formality

	n	Mean Rating	Rank
Appalachia	14	3.36	10
Cajun/Creole	4	3.00	8
Chicago	7	2.29	3
Georgia	4	3.25	9
Kentucky	6	3.50	11
Louisville/Lexington	8	2.00	1
Mid-Atlantic	7	2.43	5
Midwest	7	2.29	3
Northern	8	2.25	2
Southern	21	2.67	6
Tennessee	5	2.80	7

TABLE 3.10
Analysis of Pairings for Level of Formality

	n	Mean Rating	Rank	q	q-Critical	Significant?
Kentucky	6	3.50	11	6.115546	4.65	TRUE
Louisville/Lexington	8	2.00	1			
Kentucky	6	3.50	11	5.096288	4.65	TRUE
Northern	8	2.25	2			
Kentucky	6	3.50	11	4.80575	4.65	TRUE
Chicago	7	2.29	3			
Kentucky	6	3.50	11	4.80575	4.65	TRUE
Midwest	7	2.29	3			
Kentucky	6	3.50	11	4.240368	4.65	FALSE
Mid-Atlantic	7	2.43	5			
Appalachia	14	3.36	10	6.742339	4.65	TRUE
Louisville/Lexington	8	2.00	1			
Appalachia	14	3.36	10	5.500329	4.65	TRUE
Northern	8	2.25	2			
Appalachia	14	3.36	10	5.096288	4.65	TRUE
Chicago	7	2.29	3			
Appalachia	14	3.36	10	5.096288	4.65	TRUE
Midwest	7	2.29	3			
Appalachia	14	3.36	10	4.416783	4.65	FALSE
Mid-Atlantic	7	2.43	5			
Georgia	4	3.25	9	4.494504	4.65	FALSE
Louisville/Lexington	8	2.00	1			
Cajun/Creole	4	3.00	8	3.595603	4.65	FALSE
Louisville/Lexington	8	2.00	1			

Appalachia dialects to be statistically significantly less formal than the Lou-isville/Lexington, Northern, Chicago, and Midwest dialects. There were no other statistically significant results.

Again, as with correctness and standardness, Northern, Midwest, and Chicago dialects appear near the top of the ratings, while Appalachia, Cajun/Creole, and Georgia appear near the bottom. And while the ques-tion asks only about formality, the fact that Louisvillians are rating them-selves with or above these varieties in numerous social categories associated with prestige, taken with the fact that these areas stereotypically get associ-ated with these qualities more broadly, suggests that they are aligning them-selves with these seemingly prestigious dialects. Moreover, the fact that Lou-isvillians often rate Southern or Appalachian varieties rather low in these same dimensions, coupled with the fact that those varieties stereotypically get denigrated in these same ways more broadly, suggests Louisvillians are distancing themselves from the varieties they see as stigmatized in regards to formality and other such measures of prestige.

Table 3.11 consists of the means and rankings for how Louisvillians perceive the level of beauty among the 11 regions they have defined. Table 3.12 includes the eight different pairings involved in the analysis of level of beauty. Louisvillians perceive several varieties as the most beautiful. In this category, there was a four-way tie for most beautiful dialect among the Cajun/Creole, Mid-Atlantic, Midwest, and Southern dialects. The Georgia dialect was perceived as least beautiful. None of the results, however, were statistically significant. This result might have been inferred by the fact that all regions feature mean scores between 2 and 2.75, a rather small range of

TABLE 3.11
Summary of Level of Beauty

	n	Mean Rating	Rank
Appalachia	14	2.36	7
Cajun/Creole	4	2.00	1
Chicago	7	2.29	6
Georgia	4	2.75	11
Kentucky	6	2.67	10
Louisville/Lexington	8	2.13	5
Mid-Atlantic	7	2.00	1
Midwest	7	2.00	1
Northern	8	2.63	9
Southern	21	2.00	1
Tennessee	5	2.60	8

TABLE 3.12
Analysis of Pairings for Level of Beauty

	n	Mean Rating	Rank	q	q-Critical	Significant?
Georgia	4	2.75	11	2.492485	4.65	FALSE
Southern	21	2.00	1			
Georgia	4	2.75	11	2.16943	4.65	FALSE
Mid-Atlantic	7	2.00	1			
Georgia	4	2.75	11	2.16943	4.65	FALSE
Midwest	7	2.00	1			
Georgia	4	2.75	11	1.922994	4.65	FALSE
Cajun/Creole	4	2.00	1			
Kentucky	6	2.67	10	2.611042	4.65	FALSE
Southern	21	2.00	1			
Kentucky	6	2.67	10	2.172518	4.65	FALSE
Mid-Atlantic	7	2.00	1			
Kentucky	6	2.67	10	2.172518	4.65	FALSE
Midwest	7	2.00	1			
Kentucky	6	2.67	10	1.872475	4.65	FALSE
Cajun/Creole	4	2.00	1			

difference which suggests that beauty is not a category Louisvillians really use to distinguish varieties within this region of the United States. Such a result seems surprising, as numerous studies, beginning with Giles's work in the 1970s (e.g., Giles 1970; Giles, Bourhis, and Davies 1979; Trudgill and Giles 1978), have shown that respondents tend to create aesthetic hierarchies on a beautiful/ugly continuum.

Finally, in table 3.13, the information about how Louisvillians perceive the level of education among these regions is presented. Table 3.14 shows the three different pairings involved in the statistical analysis of level of education. As with beauty, education does not appear to be a characteristic Louisvillians use to distinguish varieties in this region of the United States. Louisvillians perceive the Northern variety as the most educated and the Tennessee variety as least educated, but none of the results of the pairings were statistically significant. This result is also fairly shocking, especially given the amount of attention the popular media places on the stereotypical notion of the stupid Southerner. Of course, if we turn to the rankings, we do find a pattern of rating varieties similar to that in other folk linguistic studies addressing the question of education; that is, Northern and Mid-

TABLE 3.13
Summary of Level of Education

	n	Mean Rating	Rank
Appalachia	14	3.14	10
Cajun/Creole	3	2.67	7
Chicago	6	2.33	4
Georgia	4	2.75	8
Kentucky	6	3.00	9
Louisville/Lexington	8	2.25	3
Mid-Atlantic	7	2.43	5
Midwest	6	2.17	2
Northern	8	1.88	1
Southern	21	2.62	6
Tennessee	5	3.20	11

TABLE 3.14
Analysis of Pairings for Level of Education

	n	Mean Rating	Rank	q	q-Critical	Significant?
Tennessee	5	3.20	11	3.594411	4.65	FALSE
Northern	8	1.88	1			
Appalachia	14	3.14	10	4.424066	4.65	FALSE
Northern	8	1.88	1			
Kentucky	6	3.00	9	3.221534	4.65	FALSE
Northern	8	1.88	1			

west varieties are rated at the top of the education scale, while Southern, Cajun/Creole, Georgia, Kentucky, Appalachia, and Tennessee round out the bottom.

In examining the individual maps, composite maps, and results of the language attitudes survey for the Louisvillians within the larger regional data set, I have shown here that Louisvillians have a rather nuanced view of linguistic variation in this smaller region of the United States. They perceive their own variety to be a separate entity, a theme that will be further explored in chapter 4, and they have determined divisions in the dialect landscape that are typically not attended to by linguists. And while the varieties that are often labeled in these kinds of tasks appear also for Louisvillians (i.e., Southern, Northern, Midwestern), these other areas (i.e., Chicago, Cajun/Creole, Tennessee) serve an important function for understanding how Louisvillians perceive variation, as exhibited through their language attitudes. For example, Louisvillians and people from Tennessee may not

actually exhibit major differences in their linguistic production, but Louisvillians choose to separate themselves from the speech of Tennesseans
because they perceive it to be uneducated, ugly, and incorrect. On the
other hand, they highly value the Midwestern and Northern varieties they
have delimited, producing the classic narrative of the educated and proper
Northerner and the dumb but pleasant Southerner in their discussion of
these varieties. As we will see in the next chapter, this discursive approach
helps Louisvillians establish for themselves a world in which their own variety is seen as consisting of the best of both worlds.

What happens, though, when Louisvillians can no longer align themselves with these areas far away from Kentucky? In the next section, we
examine how Louisvillians divide up the dialect landscape within their own
state, to see if there are ways in which their perceptions of the state impact
their perceptions of themselves.

3.3. VISION OF LANGUAGE VARIATION IN KENTUCKY

Finally, we can zoom in even further to explore how Louisvillians view the
variation they perceive in their own state. As in the previous section, I use
individual mental maps, composite maps, and language attitudes surveys
collected using the same methodologies (see chapter 1) to examine the
participants' understanding of variation. In this case, 250 participants from
across the state completed the map drawing task, of which 35 participants
were from Louisville. These maps and surveys were collected by 37 undergraduate students as part of an assignment for a course at the University of
Kentucky in the fall of 2011. The map used in this study can be found in
figure 1.7.

What we discover when the smaller map is given is that the picture
changes somewhat. While participants with the larger regional map often
left large spaces open, the tendency among Kentuckians as a whole in the
Kentucky map project was to leave little to no space within the state uncategorized. A typical map drawn by participants in that study can be seen
in figure 3.16, drawn by a 20-year-old white female Louisvillian. This map
exhibits some of the regions typically drawn by participants in this study.

Of course, there are exceptions. The map in figure 3.17 represents the
least detailed map drawn by a Louisvillian in the state-only map task. This
map was drawn by a 25-year-old white male born in Louisville and raised in
a nearby town. This drawing reveals that this participant sees nothing special about his own variety but chooses to establish the southeastern corner
of the state as a location where one finds "slow" speech, thus creating an

FIGURE 3.16
Dialect Regions Drawn by a 25-Year-Old White Male Louisvillian

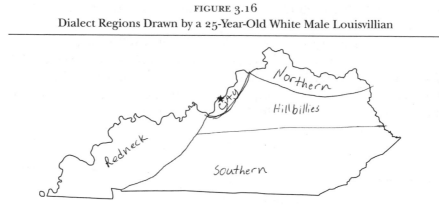

FIGURE 3.17
Least Detailed Dialect Map of Kentucky,
Drawn by a 25-Year-Old White Male Louisvillian

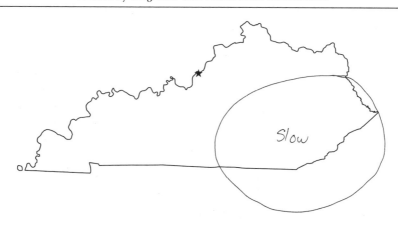

OTHER (see Bucholtz and Hall 2005) against whom he can evaluate his own speech patterns.

Some Louisvillians were willing, however, to create rather complex and elaborate pictures of variation in the state. The map in figure 3.18, drawn by a 22-year-old white male who was born in Louisville but lives in Lexington for college shows seven different varieties spread across the state. Aside from Louisville, which is geographically accurately marked, Lexington, which is perhaps slightly more north than the participant has indicated, and Ohio, which includes an area that borders that state, this participant divides the rest of the state into "Hicks," "Rednecks," "Hillbillies," and the very vague "People." Compared to other Kentuckians, this Louisvillian's view of variation in the state is much more detailed.

FIGURE 3.18
Most Detailed Dialect Map of Kentucky,
Drawn by a 22-Year-Old White Male Louisvillian

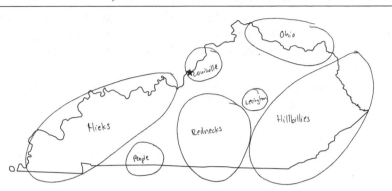

In actuality, the average Kentuckian divided the state into four or five regions. Kentuckians as a whole typically use directional labels to delimit Kentucky varieties of English. The following is a list of the overarching categories gleaned from this data set: Central Kentucky/Bluegrass, Eastern Kentucky, Northern Kentucky, Southern Kentucky, and Western Kentucky. Such labels are also present in the larger discourse about the state and can be found, for instance, in the popular media and in tourism bureau materials. This use of seemingly neutral labels is therefore unsurprising. As in the previous section, I present and discuss these regions through the use of heat maps.

I begin by discussing the Central Kentucky/Bluegrass region." In figure 3.19, we see that the core of this region is situated just to the east of

FIGURE 3.19
Composite of Central Kentucky/Bluegrass Dialect Region, Drawn by 21 Louisvillians

Louisville. The geographic label that I have chosen for an overarching category label corresponds to the fact that, as stated above, participants used the geography of the state to delimit their regional varieties of English spoken. Thus, it is not surprising that the majority of responses for this region are centered in the state. However, such a designation might suggest the geographic center of the state, yet this map seems to have a northerly inclination. Only one participant has stretched this region to the southern state line. This map partially aligns with the physiographic region known as the Bluegrass Region, known for its higher levels of Poa grass, which has blue tinted seed heads, though this physiographic region also includes the northern portion of the state. It also aligns with popular media depictions of the central portion of the state, including Louisville, as "horse country," where one finds large farms that raise thoroughbred horses and the world-famous thoroughbred race track, Churchill Downs.

The next heat map, in figure 3.20, represents the Eastern Kentucky region as delimited by Louisvillians. Again, as the label suggests, most respondents encircled the easternmost portions of the state in making their delimitations. The core of this region is just slightly west of the easternmost point in the state. The westernmost extent of the region, drawn by only one participant, is still east of the center of the state.

Figure 3.21 is the composite map for the Northern Kentucky region. In the larger discourse about Kentucky's regional divisions, Northern Kentucky is a label typically used to refer to the area of Kentucky located just south of Cincinnati, Ohio. The geographic space encompassed by this region also aligns with such a depiction, with the core of the region located just south of the Ohio River. This designation does not, however, typically

FIGURE 3.20

Composite of the Eastern Kentucky Dialect Region, Drawn by 29 Louisvillians

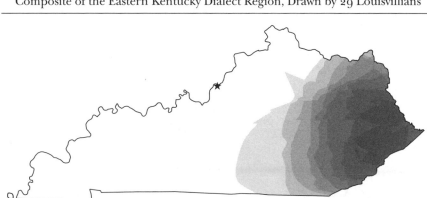

FIGURE 3.21

Composite of the Northern Kentucky Dialect Region, Drawn by 22 Louisvillians

refer to Louisville, yet at least one participant has included Louisville in this region.

The Southern Kentucky region is depicted in figure 3.22. For Kentuckians as a whole, and Louisvillians in particular, this region is the most difficult to understand. Unlike the other regions described, this dialect does not have one central core. The region expands over a larger portion of the state, and where there is agreement, it is not as consistent as in the other maps. This issue may have more to do with the analysis itself than with how participants conceive of this region. This region consists in both directional and regional labels, that is, labels referring to the geographically southern portion of the state and labels referring to areas associated with Southern

FIGURE 3.22

Composite of the Southern Kentucky Dialect Region, Drawn by 14 Louisvillians

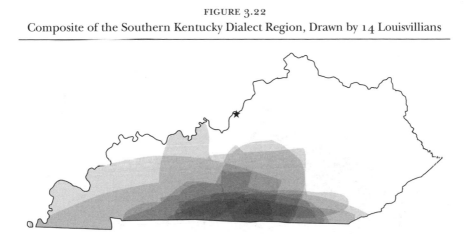

regional culture or identity. This classification did not impact the Northern Kentucky region in the same way, but it appears the word "Southern" may be being used for different purposes by different respondents. Additionally, Southern Kentucky was included because it is analogous to the other regions, but this label is not as common as the others in the popular discourses about Kentucky's regions. Finally, when analyzing the entire data set, the Southern Kentucky label did not actually meet the 14% threshold for inclusion. All of these factors complicate the issue such that one cannot be certain what this classification means for Louisvillians.

Finally, the map in figure 3.23 represents how Louisvillians envision a Western Kentucky dialect. As with the Eastern Kentucky region, this region is situated in the portion of the state that matches its label. The core of the region is near the city of Paducah, just to the east of the westernmost point in the state. The region does not stretch very far to the east, with almost all participants confining the region to the area west of Louisville.

As with the larger regional maps, I present in figure 3.24 the 50% agreement composite map for the Kentucky map project as defined by the 35 Louisvillians who participated in that study. The map is rather unsurprising. The regions, which were given directional labels, line up with the geographic areas of the state that are described by those labels. Interestingly, the Central Kentucky/Bluegrass region is confined to Louisville and its environs and does not include Frankfort, Lexington, or any of the areas outside of Louisville that more regularly have such a label applied to them in broader regional discussions of Kentucky. There is very little overlap between the regions here, with the small exception of a corner of Southern Kentucky overlapping with Western Kentucky.

FIGURE 3.23
Composite of the Western Kentucky Dialect Region, Drawn by 14 Louisvillians

FIGURE 3.24
Overall Composite Map of Louisvillians' Responses with 50% Agreement

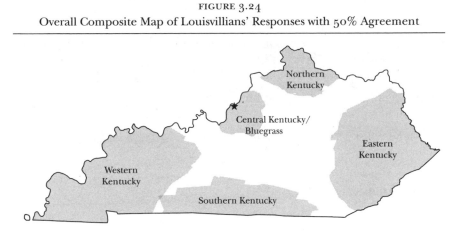

More than language, it appears cultural and geographic facts inform how Louisvillians (and Kentuckians as a whole) divide up the dialect landscape of the state. They tended to choose seemingly neutral labels that make reference to the geography of the state. Yet, while the labels may be neutral, the participants' attitudes toward them are not. In the language attitude survey that accompanied this map drawing activity, as a whole, Kentuckians rated Eastern Kentucky lowest in each of the social categories given on the language attitudes survey (i.e., correctness, pleasantness, standardness, formality, beauty, and education), while the more urban areas of Central and Northern Kentucky were rated highest. Louisvillians as a subset of this group rated these regions similarly; indeed, all rankings of Eastern Kentucky are exactly the same between Louisvillians and Kentuckians as a whole. Table 3.15 lists the information about how Louisvillians perceive the level of correctness among the five regions they have defined within the state. Table 3.16 features all 10 possible pairings involved in the analysis of level of correctness.

TABLE 3.15
Summary of Level of Correctness

	n	*Mean Rating*	*Rank*
Central Kentucky/Bluegrass	21	1 67	1
Eastern Kentucky	29	3.14	5
Northern Kentucky	22	1.95	2
Southern Kentucky	14	2.43	3
Western Kentucky	14	2.50	4

TABLE 3.16
Analysis of Pairings for Level of Correctness

	n	Mean Rating	Rank	q	q-Critical	Significant?
Eastern Kentucky	29	3.14	5	9.631681	3.92	TRUE
Central Ky./Bluegrass	21	1.67	1			
Eastern Kentucky	29	3.14	5	7.851258	3.92	TRUE
Northern Kentucky	22	1.95	2			
Eastern Kentucky	29	3.14	5	4.088679	3.92	TRUE
Southern Kentucky	14	2.43	3			
Eastern Kentucky	29	3.14	5	3.676971	3.92	FALSE
Western Kentucky	14	2.50	4			
Western Kentucky	14	2.50	4	4.530500	3.92	TRUE
Central Ky./Bluegrass	21	1.67	1			
Western Kentucky	14	2.50	4	2.992750	3.92	FALSE
Northern Kentucky	22	1.95	2			
Western Kentucky	14	2.50	4	0.354494	3.92	FALSE
Southern Kentucky	14	2.43	3			
Southern Kentucky	14	2.43	3	4.142171	3.92	TRUE
Central Ky./Bluegrass	21	1.67	1			
Southern Kentucky	14	2.43	3	2.600842	3.92	FALSE
Northern Kentucky	22	1.95	2			
Northern Kentucky	22	1.95	2	1.770044	3.92	FALSE
Central Ky./Bluegrass	21	1.67	1			

In examining the means and rankings for the level of correctness, we see that Louisvillians perceive an Eastern Kentucky dialect to be the least correct way of speaking, which is how they perceived the Appalachia region in the larger regional study, and they perceived a Central Kentucky/ Bluegrass dialect, which is where Louisvillians tend to place Louisville, to be the most correct way of speaking. These results indicate that Louisvillians believe the Eastern Kentucky dialect to be statistically significantly less correct than the Central Kentucky/Bluegrass, Northern Kentucky, and Southern Kentucky dialects. They also perceive the Western and Southern Kentucky dialects to be statistically significantly less correct than a Central Kentucky/Bluegrass dialect. There were no other statistically significant differences in level of correctness.

Table 3.17 lists the information about how Louisvillians perceive the level of pleasantness in these five regions. Table 3.18 shows the pairings

TABLE 3.17
Summary of Level of Pleasantness

	n	Mean Rating	Rank
Central Kentucky/Bluegrass	21	1.62	1
Eastern Kentucky	29	2.97	5
Northern Kentucky	22	2.00	2
Southern Kentucky	14	2.36	4
Western Kentucky	14	2.21	3

involved in the analysis of level of pleasantness. Again, Louisvillians rate Eastern Kentucky lowest and Central Kentucky/Bluegrass highest, such that the Eastern Kentucky dialect is seen as the least pleasant way of speaking and the Central Kentucky/Bluegrass dialect is the most pleasant way of speaking. These results indicate that Louisvillians believe the Eastern Ken-

TABLE 3.18
Analysis of Pairings for Level of Pleasantness

	n	Mean Rating	Rank	q	q-Critical	Significant?
Eastern Kentucky	29	2.97	5	8.004086	3.92	TRUE
Central Ky./Bluegrass	21	1.62	1			
Eastern Kentucky	29	2.97	5	5.816702	3.92	TRUE
Northern Kentucky	22	2.00	2			
Eastern Kentucky	29	2.97	5	3.931825	3.92	TRUE
Western Kentucky	14	2.21	3			
Eastern Kentucky	29	2.97	5	3.184133	3.92	FALSE
Southern Kentucky	14	2.36	4			
Southern Kentucky	14	2.36	4	3.643708	3.92	FALSE
Central Ky./Bluegrass	21	1.62	1			
Southern Kentucky	14	2.36	4	1.779335	3.92	FALSE
Northern Kentucky	22	2.00	2			
Southern Kentucky	14	2.36	4	0.643787	3.92	FALSE
Western Kentucky	14	2.21	3			
Western Kentucky	14	2.21	3	2.938474	3.92	FALSE
Central Ky./Bluegrass	21	1.62	1			
Western Kentucky	14	2.21	3	1.067601	3.92	FALSE
Northern Kentucky	22	2.00	2			
Northern Kentucky	22	2.00	2	2.126909	3.92	FALSE
Central Ky./Bluegrass	21	1.62	1			

tucky dialect to be statistically significantly less pleasant than the Central Kentucky/Bluegrass, Northern Kentucky, and Western Kentucky dialects. There were no other statistically significant differences in level of pleasantness.

Means and rankings for level of standardness for these regions are presented in table 3.19. The data involved in the statistical analysis for this

TABLE 3.19
Summary of Level of Standardness

	n	Mean Rating	Rank
Central Kentucky/Bluegrass	21	1.81	1
Eastern Kentucky	29	3.34	5
Northern Kentucky	22	1.82	2
Southern Kentucky	14	2.50	3
Western Kentucky	14	2.50	3

TABLE 3.20
Analysis of Pairings for Level of Standardness

	n	Mean Rating	Rank	q	q-Critical	Significant?
Eastern Kentucky	29	3.34	5	10.438505	3.92	TRUE
Central Ky./Bluegrass	21	1.81	1			
Eastern Kentucky	29	3.34	5	10.519228	3.92	TRUE
Northern Kentucky	22	1.82	2			
Eastern Kentucky	29	3.34	5	5.057282	3.92	TRUE
Southern Kentucky	14	2.50	3			
Eastern Kentucky	29	3.34	5	5.057282	3.92	TRUE
Western Kentucky	14	2.50	3			
Western Kentucky	14	2.50	3	3.898600	3.92	FALSE
Central Ky./Bluegrass	21	1.81	1			
Western Kentucky	14	2.50	3	3.885197	3.92	FALSE
Northern Kentucky	22	1.82	2			
Western Kentucky	14	2.50	3	0	3.92	FALSE
Southern Kentucky	14	2.50	3			
Southern Kentucky	14	2.50	3	3.898600	3.92	FALSE
Central Ky./Bluegrass	21	1.81	1			
Southern Kentucky	14	2.50	3	3.885197	3.92	FALSE
Northern Kentucky	22	1.82	2			
Northern Kentucky	22	1.82	2	2.126909	3.92	FALSE
Central Ky./Bluegrass	21	1.81	1			

category can be found in table 3.20. The same ranking of Eastern Kentucky and Central Kentucky/Bluegrass can be found here. That is, Louisvillians perceive an Eastern Kentucky dialect to be the least standard way of speaking and a Central Kentucky/Bluegrass dialect to be the most standard way of speaking. These results indicate that Louisvillians believe the Eastern Kentucky dialect to be statistically significantly less standard than all other Kentucky dialects they have delimited. There were no other statistically significant differences in level of standardness.

Information about how Louisvillians perceive level of formality for these five regions can be seen in table 3.21. Table 3.22 shows the pairings involved in the statistical analysis of level of formality. Louisvillians perceive an Eastern Kentucky dialect to be the least formal way of speaking and a Northern Kentucky dialect to be the most formal way of speaking. The fact that the top ranked dialect for this category is different than that of level of standardness means that these two categories are different for these participants. These results indicate that Louisvillians believe the Eastern Kentucky dialect to be statistically significantly less formal than all other Kentucky dialects they have delimited. Additionally, the Southern and Western Kentucky dialects are perceived to be statistically significantly less formal than a Northern Kentucky and a Central Kentucky/Bluegrass dialect. There were no other statistically significant differences in level of formality.

Table 3.23 includes the information about how Louisvillians perceive the level of beauty among the regions they have defined within the state. All ten possible pairings in the analysis for this category are presented in table 3.24. Here we return to the typical ratings wherein Eastern Kentucky is rated lowest and Central Kentucky/Bluegrass is rated highest. Louisvillians perceive an Eastern Kentucky dialect to be the least beautiful way of speaking and a Central Kentucky/Bluegrass dialect to be the most beautiful way of speaking. These results indicate that Louisvillians believe the Eastern Kentucky dialect to be statistically significantly less beautiful than a Central Kentucky/Bluegrass dialect and a Northern Kentucky dialect. There were no other statistically significant differences in level of beauty.

Finally, the summary of information about how Louisvillians perceive level of education in the state is presented in table 3.25. Table 3.26 features the statistical analysis of this data for level of education. Louisvillians perceive an Eastern Kentucky dialect to be the least educated way of speaking and a Central Kentucky/Bluegrass dialect to be the most educated way of speaking. These results indicate that Louisvillians believe the Eastern Kentucky dialect to be statistically significantly less educated than a Central Kentucky/Bluegrass, Northern Kentucky, and Southern Kentucky dialect. Also, Western and Southern Kentucky dialects were rated statistically

TABLE 3.21
Summary of Level of Formality

	n	Mean Rating	Rank
Central Kentucky/Bluegrass	21	2.14	2
Eastern Kentucky	29	3.72	5
Northern Kentucky	22	2.05	1
Southern Kentucky	14	2.93	4
Western Kentucky	14	2.86	3

TABLE 3.22
Analysis of Pairings for Level of Formality

	n	Mean Rating	Rank	q	q-Critical	Significant?
Eastern Kentucky	29	3.72	5	12.071791	3.92	TRUE
Northern Kentucky	22	2.05	1			
Eastern Kentucky	29	3.72	5	11.220450	3.92	TRUE
Central Ky./Bluegrass	21	2.14	2			
Eastern Kentucky	29	3.72	5	5.416554	3.92	TRUE
Western Kentucky	14	2.86	3			
Eastern Kentucky	29	3.72	5	4.970304	3.92	TRUE
Southern Kentucky	14	2.93	4			
Southern Kentucky	14	2.93	4	5.251942	3.92	TRUE
Northern Kentucky	22	2.05	1			
Southern Kentucky	14	2.93	4	4.630010	3.92	TRUE
Central Ky./Bluegrass	21	2.14	2			
Southern Kentucky	14	2.93	4	0.384237	3.92	FALSE
Western Kentucky	14	2.86	3			
Western Kentucky	14	2.86	3	4.827153	3.92	TRUE
Northern Kentucky	22	2.05	1			
Western Kentucky	14	2.86	3	4.209100	3.92	TRUE
Central Ky./Bluegrass	21	2.14	2			
Central Ky./Bluegrass	21	2.14	2	0.649135	3.92	FALSE
Northern Kentucky	22	2.05	1			

significantly less educated than both a Central Kentucky/Bluegrass and a Northern Kentucky dialect. There were no other statistically significant differences in level of education.

The evaluations given in the Kentucky map project in some ways mirror those from the larger regional map drawing task. For instance, Appalachia

TABLE 3.23
Summary of Level of Beauty

	n	Mean Rating	Rank
Central Kentucky/Bluegrass	21	2.19	1
Eastern Kentucky	29	3.17	5
Northern Kentucky	22	2.41	2
Southern Kentucky	14	2.57	3
Western Kentucky	14	2.57	3

TABLE 3.24
Analysis of Pairings for Level of Beauty

	n	Mean Rating	Rank	q	q-Critical	Significant?
Eastern Kentucky	29	3.17	5	5.925458	3.92	TRUE
Central Ky./Bluegrass	21	2.19	1			
Eastern Kentucky	29	3.17	5	4.668184	3.92	TRUE
Northern Kentucky	22	2.41	2			
Eastern Kentucky	29	3.17	5	3.193059	3.92	FALSE
Southern Kentucky	14	2.57	3			
Eastern Kentucky	29	3.17	5	3.193059	3.92	FALSE
Western Kentucky	14	2.57	3			
Western Kentucky	14	2.57	3	1.909083	3.92	FALSE
Central Ky./Bluegrass	21	2.19	1			
Western Kentucky	14	2.57	3	0.821028	3.92	FALSE
Northern Kentucky	22	2.41	2			
Western Kentucky	14	2.57	3	0	3.92	FALSE
Southern Kentucky	14	2.57	3			
Southern Kentucky	14	2.57	3	1.909083	3.92	FALSE
Central Ky./Bluegrass	21	2.19	1			
Southern Kentucky	14	2.57	3	0.821028	3.92	FALSE
Northern Kentucky	22	2.41	2			
Northern Kentucky	22	2.41	2	1.239026	3.92	FALSE
Central Ky./Bluegrass	21	2.19	1			

in the regional map, which was mostly confined to the eastern portion of Kentucky, was rated rather poorly in all social characteristics on the survey that accompanied the regional map, just as the Eastern Kentucky region was in the state-only study. These ratings can be attributed to Louisvillians choosing to distance themselves from the stereotypes that are applied to

TABLE 3.25
Summary of Level of Education

	n	Mean Rating	Rank
Central Kentucky/Bluegrass	21	1.81	1
Eastern Kentucky	29	3.34	5
Northern Kentucky	22	1.82	2
Southern Kentucky	14	2.57	3
Western Kentucky	14	2.71	4

TABLE 3.26
Analysis of Pairings for Level of Education

	n	Mean Rating	Rank	q	q-Critical	Significant?
Eastern Kentucky	29	3.34	5	10.306661	3.92	TRUE
Central Ky./Bluegrass	21	1.81	1			
Eastern Kentucky	29	3.34	5	10.386697	3.92	TRUE
Northern Kentucky	22	1.82	2			
Eastern Kentucky	29	3.34	5	4.571370	3.92	TRUE
Southern Kentucky	14	2.57	3			
Eastern Kentucky	29	3.34	5	3.726976	3.92	FALSE
Western Kentucky	14	2.71	4			
Western Kentucky	14	2.71	4	5.044149	3.92	TRUE
Central Ky./Bluegrass	21	1.81	1			
Western Kentucky	14	2.71	4	5.041925	3.92	TRUE
Northern Kentucky	22	1.82	2			
Western Kentucky	14	2.71	4	0.727051	3.92	FALSE
Southern Kentucky	14	2.57	3			
Southern Kentucky	14	2.57	3	4.247704	3.92	TRUE
Central Ky./Bluegrass	21	1.81	1			
Southern Kentucky	14	2.57	3	4.238140	3.92	TRUE
Northern Kentucky	22	1.82	2			
Northern Kentucky	22	1.82	2	0.054591	3.92	FALSE
Central Ky./Bluegrass	21	1.81	1			

such a region. Indeed, these low ratings sound quite similar to Preston's (1989) Southern Indiana results, which he described as follows:

That the American South takes last place in correctness from the point of view of these [southern Indiana] respondents may be, at least in part, an act of frightened dissociation. [...] [T]he desire of residents from the southern part of the state to dissociate themselves from the traditional or even border South is strong. In fact, one of the most striking findings in this study is the Kentucky-Indiana difference. [...] [T]he southern Indiana respondents of this study see their Kentucky neighbors as members of the nonstandard South and themselves as part of the standard North Central region. [56]

These Louisvillians can be said to be doing the same to the other residents of their state. The rural and mountain rural areas within Kentucky are typically placed in the same dialect region as Louisville, so to separate themselves from the perceptions of nonstandard and incorrect speech, they choose to rate the varieties very close to them very low.

This is also accomplished by classifying Louisville as a Central Kentucky/Bluegrass variety, which was rated very highly in the surveys. The higher ratings for this region and for Northern Kentucky can be attributed to their association with urban areas. Fridland and Bartlett (2006) suggest that larger cities are often associated with prestige, which results in these areas having higher rankings. Louisvillians see their own city as worthy of such prestige, giving the region that encompasses the city the highest ratings in almost all categories. In the analysis of these data, I have shown that the rural/urban divide is a strong feature in how Louisvillians define the dialect landscape of their state (see also Cramer 2016).

3.4. DISCUSSION

This chapter has examined how Louisvillians understand the dialect landscape of the United States as a whole, of the larger region surrounding Kentucky, and of the state of Kentucky by using a perceptual dialectology framework for data collection and analysis. I have shown how regional variation is perceived by Louisvillians by exploring their mental maps, composite maps, and language attitudes, thus establishing the categories that Louisvillians use to talk about dialectal variation and the sentiments they hold with respect to that variation, which begins to show which varieties Louisvillians hold in high esteem and which ones are denigrated.

One point shown in this chapter is that Louisvillians, like others who have completed such tasks, have a more nuanced view of variation when the area under investigation is smaller (e.g., Benson 2003; Bucholtz et al. 2007; Bucholtz et al. 2008). The ideologies about variation became more precise as we moved from the broader picture of the United States, in which Louisvillians painted a picture of equality, to the regional map, in which 11 different varieties were delimited, to the Kentucky map, in which the entire state was usually categorized in some way. The argument is one of proximity

(Montgomery 2012), such that Louisvillians are more comfortable producing maps/attitudes about areas that are more proximate.

In the next chapter, I explore much of these same data further to show how Louisvillians construct a specific regional identity for their city by more specifically analyzing where they place Louisville in their mental maps and how they evaluate the city in terms of their language attitudes.

4. LOCATING LOUISVILLE

Having established how Louisvillians perceive the dialect landscape at the national, regional, and state level, it is possible to explore more specifically how they categorize their own city. In particular, I am concerned with where Louisvillians place their city in terms of its regional and state location and with how they evaluate certain varieties in terms of various social characterizations, therefore choosing to align or disalign with those varieties by the attitudes they exhibit toward them.

The maps and attitudes data explored in this chapter are the same as those encountered in chapter 3, with the focus turned on the placement of Louisville in the dialect landscape. To answer the question of physical location, I examine several individual mental maps, taken from the larger regional study as well as the Kentucky study, and some composite maps, to show that Louisville is often depicted as located at some kind of border, as separate or uncategorized, or as "a place between places" (Llamas 2007). I explore how Louisvillians rate other varieties in terms of degree of difference and once again return to their attitudes toward certain varieties to determine with which groups of speakers Louisvillians identify and those from whom they dissociate.

In what follows I show the ways in which the border has impacted Louisvillians in their construction of regional linguistic identities. Namely, the results suggest that while Louisville is mapped in varying ways, Louisvillians prefer to take a "best-of-both-worlds" approach to their own identities, choosing to align with whichever region they perceive to be more prestigious for any given social characteristic.

4.1. THE MANY WAYS OF MAPPING LOUISVILLE

We begin by exploring how Louisville is represented in the larger regional mental maps (see figure 1.6). As with Preston's Southern Indiana participants (e.g., Preston 1989), many Louisvillians chose not to classify their city at all on their individual maps. An example of this can be seen in figure 4.1. This map, created by a 35-year-old white female who reported to have lived her entire life in Louisville, includes only two regions: a Southern region and an Appalachian region. With the exception of the eastern part of Kentucky, geographically appropriately labeled Appalachian, this partici-

FIGURE 4.1
Dialect Regions Drawn by a 35-Year-Old White Female Louisvillian

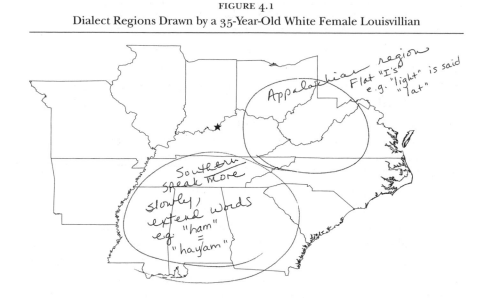

pant left the entire state, not just Louisville, without designation, possibly indicating her difficulty in determining the appropriate regional label for this area.

As discussed in chapter 3, many participants selected Louisville (or Louisville and Lexington) as a separate region (see, e.g., figure 3.6). In figure 4.2, we see that the participant, a 38-year-old white male born and raised in Louisville, has delineated a Southern region that just barely reaches the boundaries of a region encompassing only Louisville, which he has labeled "Mid Southern/Midwest," a label that most certainly points to his complex understanding of Louisville's regional classification. This participant seems to be claiming that Louisville is both Southern and Midwestern, which highlights the border nature of the city. The outer border of the Northern Midwest region on his map also just barely reaches the boundaries of this separate Louisville region, thus positioning Louisville as a place between places.

In figure 4.3, we can start to see an actual border running through Louisville, though it is unclear what might be on the other side of the line. This 23-year-old white female, who has lived her entire life in Louisville, drew the northern boundary of her Southern region almost through the city of Louisville. She makes no designation about the region on the immediate other side, but her delimitation of Southern indicates an uncertainty about where Louisville belongs. No further information was gleaned about this

FIGURE 4.2
Dialect Regions Drawn by a 38-Year-Old White Male Louisvillian

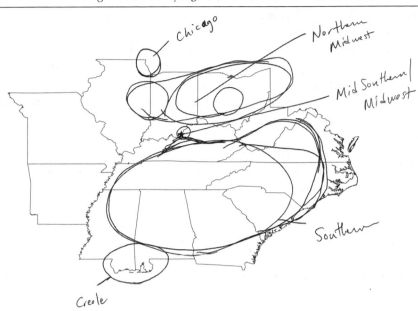

FIGURE 4.3
Dialect Regions Drawn by a 23-Year-Old White Female Louisvillian

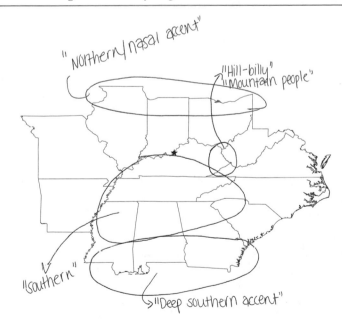

category from her answers to the open-ended questions; however, she mentions that this dialect is noted for its "long 'i's," which partially coincides with Labov, Ash, and Boberg's (2006) definition of the South in terms of /aɪ/ monophthongization.

This struggle in the regional classification of Louisville is made most clear in figure 4.4. This map, created by a 37-year-old white female who was born in Louisville and spent a short period of time elsewhere for college, features two wavy lines, indicating that the line between Southern and Midwestern is blurred for this participant, particularly through the Louisville area.[1]

Based on these maps, it seems that the major debate about Louisville's position seems to be either about Louisville as a Southern or Midwestern/Northern city. However, some participants presented other interpretations. In figure 4.5, Louisville is presented as possibly on the border between a "Midwestern accent" and a "Beginning Northern accent," technically falling into both categories, as in figure 4.4, but with no possibility for interpretation of Louisville as Southern. For the participant who created figure 4.6, Louisville seems to be connected to the speech of the mostly Appalachian area, which others described as distinct.

FIGURE 4.4
Dialect Region Drawn by a 37-Year-Old White Female Louisvillian

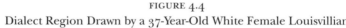

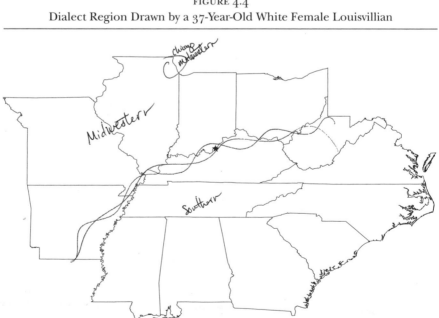

FIGURE 4.5
Louisville as Distinctly Non-Southern, Drawn by a 61-Year-Old
White Male Louisvillian

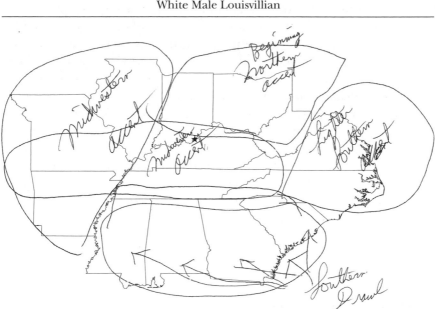

FIGURE 4.6
Louisville as Marginally Appalachian, Drawn by a 30-Year-Old
White Male Louisvillian

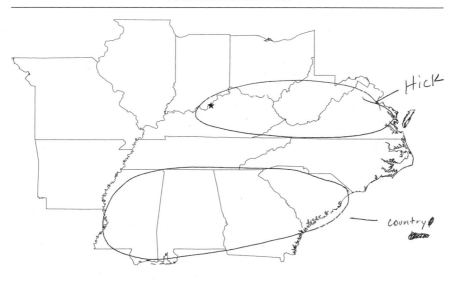

In chapter 3, Louisville/Lexington was considered as its own independent region, but many participants in the regional map task chose instead to place Louisville within other regions, indicating the regional placement they perceive for the city. The heat maps for three of these regions, Southern, Midwest, and Northern, are presented here (see chapter 3 for heat maps for other regions). These regions are often considered by Louisvillians in the determination of Louisville's location in the dialect landscape. Figure 4.7 is the delimitation of the Midwest region. This region is described mostly as a neutral, correct, or standard way of speaking, connecting the speech here rather stereotypically to the speech of newscasters. There appear to be two cores for this region: one in east central Illinois and western Indiana and another in east central Missouri and western Illinois. For at least one participant, the Midwest region extends as far south as Mississippi, Tennessee, and North Carolina, and the overall region encompasses most of Ohio and the entirety of Arkansas, Missouri, Illinois, Indiana, and Kentucky. Only two participants included Louisville in the Midwest region, with one of those participants drawing the cut-off right through the Louisville area. So for the majority of respondents, Louisville is not a Midwestern city, though an examination of other regions will reveal that perhaps Louisville has no real clear regional position.

FIGURE 4.7
Composite of the Midwest Dialect Region, Drawn by 7 Louisvillians

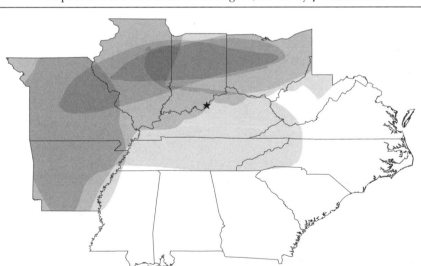

Figure 4.8 is the delimitation of the Northern dialect area by Louisvillians. This dialect is represented rather negatively, including descriptions of
"Northern inhospitality" and of shortness defined as "snippy," "stuffy," and
"rude." Given that no "real" Northern states (i.e., states in the northeast or
New England) appear on this map, Louisville respondents chose Ohio as
the representative of this dialect. This is similar to how respondents represented the Cajun/Creole dialect on their maps, despite the fact that Louisiana was not given on the map. Three rather small cores are defined for
the Northern region, all within the state of Ohio, though the region spans
as far west as Illinois and as far south as northern Kentucky. No participants
in this study included Louisville within this region, with one participant explicitly explaining that a Northern dialect is one that is "north of the Ohio
river and east of Louisville." Another participant suggested that the speech
was no different in Louisville than it was in the Northern region, yet she
did not include Louisville in her Northern region. It appears, then, that
Louisvillians also do not see themselves as Northern, though the southern
border of this region, for at least one participant, comes quite close.

Lastly, we consider the Southern dialect region, which was represented
in 21 participant maps and can be seen in figure 4.9. This was the most
frequently defined region (overall and among Louisvillians), and, unlike

FIGURE 4.8
Composite of the Northern Dialect Region, Drawn by 8 Louisvillians

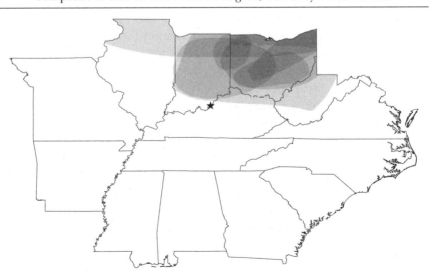

FIGURE 4.9

Composite of the Southern Dialect Region, Drawn by 21 Louisvillians

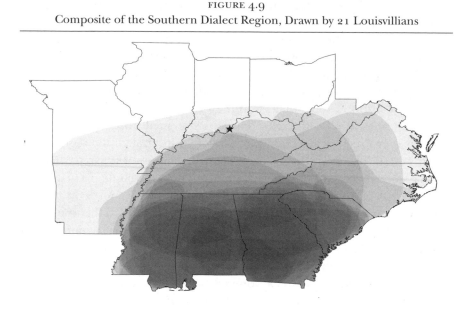

many of the other regions, Louisvillians described the Southern region in generally pleasant terms, frequently using words such as "friendly," "calm," "happy," and "down-to-earth" to describe it. As the most frequently defined region, it spans the largest part of the map, including all or parts of every state on the map. There are several cores for this region, all located in Georgia and Alabama. Louisville is only included as part of the Southern region in two maps, while another delimitation for the South comes just south of the Louisville area. In this sense, just like with the Midwest region, Louisville is not considered to be a Southern city by the majority of Louisvillians, despite the fact that they seem to value this variety more than others.

The outcome of exploring both the individual and composite regional maps, with respect to Louisville's placement, seems to be that Louisville is considered either to be its own dialect, as represented in chapter 3 by the Louisville/Lexington region, or as a place between places with no real regional affiliation. Perhaps the fact that Louisville is both one of the largest cities south of the Ohio River and is located in a rather rural state makes selecting the appropriate regional distinction difficult. Yet, participants had no difficulty including cities like Atlanta, Georgia, and Birmingham, Alabama, in the Southern region. Similarly, participants easily classified Indianapolis, Indiana, and Cleveland, Ohio, as belonging to either the Midwestern or Northern regions, respectively. These cities were not left unmarked because of their urbanity. It seems clear that Louisvillians experience their own city as being located at some border, not clearly belonging to any of the typically defined regions of the United States.

In returning to the state-only maps, where participants could only position Louisville within the state itself, we find additional issues with consistency in terms of Louisville's position. Typically respondents in this data set divided the state into four or five very large regions covering the majority of the state. The map in figure 4.10 is one such map. For this participant, the area labeled "'normal' city talk" includes the city of Louisville (as indicated by the location of the star). The most common way in which Louisville was categorized in maps was in this way, such that the geography and the discussion of the label aligned Louisville with Lexington and the rest of Central Kentucky. Therefore, when participants chose to place Louisville within a region, it was most often placed within the Central Kentucky region.

Some participants, however, aligned the city more with Northern Kentucky, as seen in figure 4.11. This map, which may have also included Lexington in the Northern Kentucky region, showcases what is often called the "Golden Triangle" in popular discourses of Kentucky (see Tenkotte and Claypool 2009). The triangle, with Louisville, Lexington, and the greater Cincinnati area serving as the three points, represents an area of higher economic growth and development within the state. As we saw in the pre-

FIGURE 4.10
Louisville as Part of Central Kentucky, Drawn by a 19-Year-Old
White Male Louisvillian

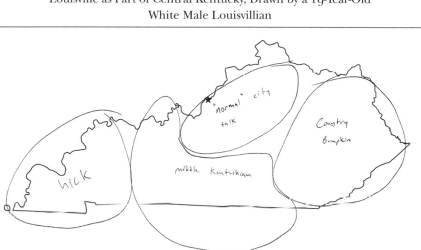

FIGURE 4.11
Louisville as Part of Northern Kentucky, Drawn by a 20-Year-Old
White Male Louisvillian

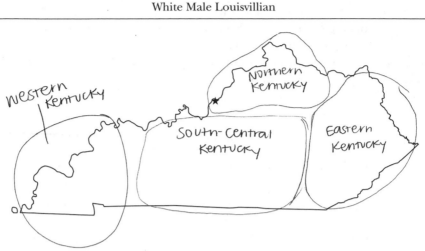

vious chapter, both Central Kentucky and Northern Kentucky get linked to positive traits like education and formality, such that this area seems to represent a linguistic "Golden Triangle" as well.

As the map in figure 4.1 showed in the larger region, Louisvillians also sometimes chose to not classify Louisville at all, even within the state. An example of this phenomenon can be seen in figure 4.12. This participant, a 50-year-old white female from Louisville, made a distinction between the eastern and western portions of the state, both substantially rural areas,

FIGURE 4.12
Louisville as Uncategorized, Drawn by a 50-Year-Old White Female Louisvillian

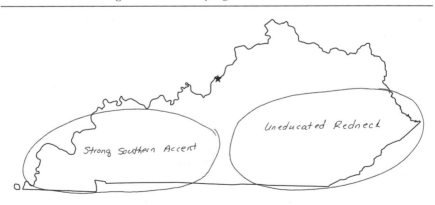

without making any reference to or categorization of the more urban areas of Louisville, Lexington, and the greater Cincinnati area. For this participant, then, the important linguistic variation in the state is not between rural and urban areas but between two different kinds of rural.

Finally, another way in which Louisville was categorized by Louisvillians was as a region in and of itself. This was also true in the larger regional study, as evidenced by the presence of the Louisville/Lexington region discussed in chapter 3. The map in figure 4.13 (cf. figure 3.16 and figure 3.18) shows a fairly accurate delimitation of the greater Louisville area as drawn by this participant. The map showcases another common phenomenon as well: this participant has only circled Louisville and a portion of Appalachian Kentucky. In previous work (e.g., Cramer 2011), I have shown that this juxtaposition of Louisville with Appalachia serves an important role for Louisvillians. Namely, creating this juxtaposition with Appalachia allows Louisvillians to distinguish themselves from an area in the state that has been subjected to more negative stereotypes in the wider national discourse (e.g., popular Hollywood films like *Deliverance*)—ones from which Louisvillians wish to distance themselves.

The picture of variation in the state that was shown in the previous chapter (figure 3.24), reproduced here as figure 4.14. What we see in terms of the regional placement of Louisville is that the primary consideration for Louisville's placement in the state is that it belongs to Central Kentucky. As we will see in the next chapter, non-Louisvillians in the state do not exactly agree with this designation. Indeed, in the popular discourses about Louisville's location in the state, there is some debate: Central Kentucky typi-

FIGURE 4.13
Louisville as Separate, Drawn by a 23-Year-Old
White Male Louisvillian

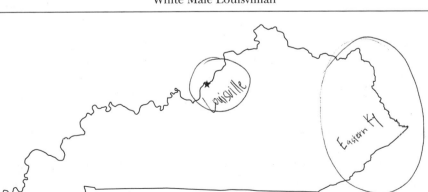

FIGURE 4.14

Overall Composite Map of Louisvillians' Responses with 50% Agreement

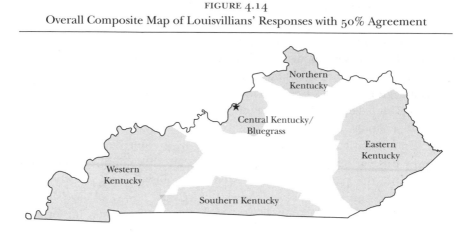

cally refers to Lexington and its environs, while Northern Kentucky refers to the areas in the state just across the river from Cincinnati, Ohio. Eastern Kentucky is described as the area containing the Appalachians, which places the entire area east of Lexington, yet Western Kentucky seems to start somewhere to the west of Louisville, thus leaving Louisville without regional depiction in that discourse. Perhaps this fact explains why many Louisvillians left their city without designation or chose to encircle it as its own region. It appears, then, that Louisvillians' understandings of Kentucky's linguistic variation are highly informed by their understandings of other kinds of regional variation present within the state as well.

This section has shown that there are varying interpretations about where Louisville is located in the dialect landscape of the region and the state. While some participants squarely place Louisville in one region or another, many choose to make it a separate region altogether and others present rather blurry boundaries in the vicinity of the city. I argue that Louisville's specific geopolitical, sociohistorical position at a border causes such confusion. In addition to the disagreement seen in terms of where to position Louisville in these maps, a discussion of their sentiments toward other varieties reveals that this border mentality impacts the ways in which they socially categorize the city as well. In what follows, I examine several aspects of their language attitudes that showcase how Louisvillians attempt to take a "best-of-both-worlds" approach to describing linguistic variation with respect to their own variety. I begin this discussion by exploring how

Louisvillians rate other varieties in terms of how different they are from a Louisville variety.

4.2. DEGREES OF DIFFERENCE

In the previous chapter, we saw the ways in which Louisvillians discussed levels of correctness and pleasantness among the 50 states, Washington, D.C., and New York City by examining data from an online survey. That survey also asked participants to rate those same states and cities in terms of how different it was from their own way of speaking. In this section, I present the ratings given by Louisvillians in this degree of difference task. Recall that a lower score in this task indicates a lower level of difference, such that states and cities with low scores are thought to be least different from (i.e., most similar to) the respondent's speech.[2]

The choropleth map in figure 4.15 represents the average ratings of the states by the 35 Louisvillians who took part in this survey. The darkest color represents the varieties that are perceived to be most similar to a Louisvillian's way of speaking; in this case, Kentucky, Indiana, and Ohio are rated as most similar. In actuality, Indiana was rated as more similar to Louisville speech than Kentucky (though by a very small margin; Indiana's average rating was 1.57 while Kentucky's was 1.69). Louisiana was rated as most different at 3.11 and is grouped with New Jersey, Ney York, New York City, Connecticut, Massachusetts, Minnesota, and Alabama.

TABLE 4.15
Louisvillians' Degree of Difference Ratings

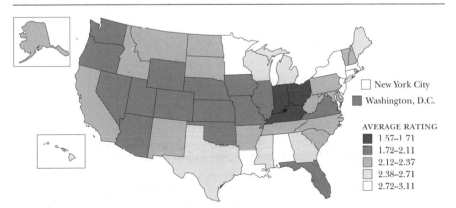

This map reveals similar sentiments as the correctness and pleasantness ratings. For example, Louisvillians rated New Jersey as very incorrect and unpleasant; as such, Louisvillians do not want to associate their own speech with that variety and have therefore rated it as very different from their own speech. Interestingly, Indiana and Ohio, which were rated as very similar, were rated as both more correct and less pleasant than Kentucky speech. It also appears that Louisvillians see their speech as quite different from states in the Upper North. This fact is confirmed by an examination of the regional means based on the regional divisions outlined in Fridland and Bartlett (2006), as presented in chapter 3 (see figure 3.3). Those averages can be found in table 4.1. This chart also reveals that Louisvillians are more likely to say that their own speech is most similar to the Midland states.

Unlike the correctness and pleasantness results, the differences calculated between regions was statistically significant for level of difference. The information in table 4.2 shows the results of a one-way analysis of variance (ANOVA) calculated on participants' ratings of degree of difference, revealing that the differences are significant at $p = .001$, $F(4, 160) = 4.75$. Thus, while Louisvillians did not provide ratings for levels of correctness and pleasantness in a way to reveal that they perceive any regional variety to be particularly more or less correct or pleasant, they do use degree of difference as a way of differentiating varieties.

Beyond these individual ratings of states and the two cities and the combined regional ratings in terms of degree of difference, we can also return to the language attitudes survey data that stem from the regional

TABLE 4.1
Average Ratings of Difference by Region

	Mean Rating	Rank
South	2.30	3
Upper North	2.58	5
Midland	1.94	1
West	2.09	2
Other	2.34	4

TABLE 4.2
ANOVA Results for Level of Difference

Source of Variation	Sum of Squares	df	Mean Square	F	p-Value
Difference					
Between groups	8.91207	4	2.228018	4.746008	0.001179
Within groups	79.8068	160	0.469451		
TOTAL	88.71875	164			

TABLE 4.3
Summary of Level of Difference

	n	Mean Rating	Rank
Appalachia	14	2.86	9
Cajun/Creole	4	3.75	11
Chicago	7	2.43	3
Georgia	4	2.50	5
Kentucky	6	2.67	6
Louisville/Lexington	8	1.38	1
Mid-Atlantic	7	2.43	3
Midwest	7	2.14	2
Northern	8	2.75	8
Southern	21	2.67	6
Tennessee	5	3.20	10

map drawing task wherein degree of difference ratings were assigned to the dialect areas drawn by participants in that task (see chapter 3 for a discussion of the other social characteristics included on that survey). Table 4.3 lists the information about the level of difference Louisvillians perceive between their own way of speaking and the 11 overarching categories they defined. Table 4.4 features the 13 different pairings involved in the analysis of level of difference.

Looking at the means and rankings for the level of difference in the regions from the language attitudes survey that accompanied the regional map task, Louisvillians perceive a Cajun/Creole dialect to be the most different from their own way of speaking and a Louisville/Lexington dialect as most similar to their own way of speaking. These results indicate that Louisvillians believe the Cajun/Creole, Tennessee, Appalachian, Northern, and Southern dialects to be statistically significantly more different from their own way of speaking than a Louisville/Lexington dialect, a result which seems quite intuitive given that most respondents who identified a specific Louisville/Lexington dialect almost necessarily identified it as not different from their own way of speaking since they are from Louisville. There were no other statistically significant differences; that is, no other variety was thought to be statistically significantly more different from their own way of speaking than another other variety. Thus, as one might expect, a Kentucky dialect is not statistically significantly different from a Louisville/Lexington dialect, even though the rankings themselves are quite different.

What is interesting to note in these results is that while Louisvillians do see a statistically significant difference between their own variety and a Southern variety, there was no significant difference between a Louisville/

TABLE 4.4
Analysis of Pairings for Level of Diffference

	n	Mean Rating	Rank	q	q-Critical	Significant?
Cajun/Creole	4	3.75	11	6.943028	4.65	TRUE
Louisville/Lexington	8	1.38	1			
Cajun/Creole	4	3.75	11	4.590269	4.65	FALSE
Midwest	7	2.14	2			
Tennessee	5	3.20	10	5.730891	4.65	TRUE
Louisville/Lexington	8	1.38	1			
Tennessee	5	3.20	10	3.232050	4.65	FALSE
Midwest	7	2.14	2			
Appalachia	14	2.86	9	5.986716	4.65	TRUE
Louisville/Lexington	8	1.38	1			
Appalachia	14	2.86	9	2.762335	4.65	FALSE
Midwest	7	2.14	2			
Northern	8	2.75	8	4.923043	4.65	TRUE
Louisville/Lexington	8	1.38	1			
Northern	8	2.75	8	2.100101	4.65	FALSE
Midwest	7	2.14	2			
Southern	21	2.67	6	5.565537	4.65	TRUE
Louisville/Lexington	8	1.38	1			
Southern	21	2.67	6	2.148592	4.65	FALSE
Midwest	7	2.14	2			
Kentucky	6	2.67	6	4.281619	4.65	FALSE
Louisville/Lexington	8	1.38	1			
Kentucky	6	2.67	6	1.685494	4.65	FALSE
Midwest	7	2.14	2			
Georgia	4	2.50	5	3.288803	4.65	FALSE
Louisville/Lexington	8	1.38	1			

Lexington dialect and a Midwest dialect.[3] In fact, these two varieties were rated as the least and second least different varieties, respectively. Thus, it appears that, at least in level of difference, Louisvillians align themselves more closely with a Midwest way of speaking than with a Southern one. That is, when rating Louisville, the Midwest, and the South, Louisvillians rate Louisville in a way so that it is seen as less different than the Midwest than it is the South.

Finally, we similarly return to the degree of difference ratings included in the language attitudes survey that accompanied the state-only map drawing task, using the overarching categories that were established in that task (see chapter 3 for a discussion of the other social characteristics included on that survey). As we saw in the previous chapter, Eastern Kentucky was rated lowest in each of the social characteristics evaluated, and the Central Kentucky/Bluegrass and Northern Kentucky regions were rated highest. The same is true in terms of degree of difference where Kentuckians as a whole and Louisvillians specifically rank the varieties in exactly the same way, as seen in table 4.5.

Information about how Louisvillians in the state-only data set perceive the level of difference among the five regions they have depicted can be seen in table 4.6. The statistical analysis of this data is in table 4.7, which shows the 10 possible pairings involved in the analysis of level of difference. Louisvillians perceive an Eastern Kentucky dialect to be the most different way of speaking. Indeed, this is similar to the results of the larger regional study, where Appalachia was rated as rather different from a Louisville/ Lexington variety. Participants perceived a Central Kentucky/Bluegrass dialect to be the least different way of speaking. This result is unsurprising given that this is the region where most Louisvillians placed Louisville in the map drawing task. These results indicate that Louisvillians believe the Eastern Kentucky dialect to be statistically significantly more different than all other regional dialects. They also perceive the Western and Southern Kentucky dialects to be statistically significantly more different than a Central Kentucky/Bluegrass dialect and the Southern Kentucky dialect to

TABLE 4.5
Rankings of Difference by Regions by Louisvillians and Kentuckians

	Louisvillians	Kentuckians
Central Kentucky/Bluegrass	1	1
Eastern Kentucky	5	5
Northern Kentucky	2	2
Southern Kentucky	3	3
Western Kentucky	4	4

TABLE 4.6
Summary of Level of Difference

	n	Mean Rating	Rank
Central Kentucky/Bluegrass	21	1.43	1
Eastern Kentucky	29	3.69	5
Northern Kentucky	22	2.14	2
Southern Kentucky	14	2.86	4
Western Kentucky	14	2.71	3

TABLE 4.7
Analysis of Pairings for Level of Difference

	n	Mean Rating	Rank	q	q-Critical	Significant?
Eastern Kentucky	29	3.69	5	15.949026	3.92	TRUE
Central Ky./Bluegrass	21	1.43	1			
Eastern Kentucky	29	3.69	5	11.103812	3.92	TRUE
Northern Kentucky	22	2.14	2			
Eastern Kentucky	29	3.69	5	6.057478	3.92	TRUE
Western Kentucky	14	2.71	3			
Eastern Kentucky	29	3.69	5	5.170271	3.92	TRUE
Southern Kentucky	14	2.86	4			
Southern Kentucky	14	2.86	4	8.368266	3.92	TRUE
Central Ky./Bluegrass	21	1.43	1			
Southern Kentucky	14	2.86	4	4.261085	3.92	TRUE
Northern Kentucky	22	2.14	2			
Southern Kentucky	14	2.86	4	0.763915	3.92	FALSE
Western Kentucky	14	2.71	3			
Western Kentucky	14	2.71	3	7.531439	3.92	TRUE
Central Ky./Bluegrass	21	1.43	1			
Western Kentucky	14	2.71	3	3.416546	3.92	FALSE
Northern Kentucky	22	2.14	2			
Northern Kentucky	22	2.14	2	4.689067	3.92	TRUE
Central Ky./Bluegrass	21	1.43	1			

be statistically significantly more different than a Northern Kentucky dialect. Finally, the Northern Kentucky dialect was perceived to be statistically significantly more different than the Central Kentucky/Bluegrass dialect as well. There were no other statistically significant differences in level of difference.

All in all, this section has shown that while Louisvillians tend to align themselves more closely with Midwestern varieties in the regional map task, they do not fully distance themselves from the South. Their ratings indicate that they believe varieties in the Upper North to be most different, whereas Southern varieties were often rated in the middle. Within the state, Louisvillians align with the more urban areas of Northern and Central Kentucky, choosing to separate themselves from the more rural parts of the state. Interestingly, the area that Louisvillians distanced themselves from in both map drawing activities was the Appalachian region. This area is perceived to be very different than a Louisville way of speaking, and as we will see in the next section, Appalachia is seen as a bastion of badness for Louisvillians. As such, Louisvillians use the low ratings of this region to distance themselves from that area in many social characteristics, but they also seem to embrace many of the more positive characteristics they associate with Southernness.

4.3. ATTITUDES AND BELONGING

In chapter 3, we explored how Louisvillians rated the many varieties they delimited in the larger regional study and the Kentucky study to show how they viewed regional variation rather broadly. In this section, I return to those attitudes to examine specifically how they evaluate Louisville speech. In so doing, we can get a glimpse of how Louisvillians perceive their own city in terms of regional belonging. I begin with an exploration of the data gleaned from the regional map study. A summation of the rankings of each region for each social characteristic can be found in table 4.8.

In terms of correctness, the Louisville/Lexington dialect was rated as being between the Northern and the Southern dialects, with Midwest and Chicago tied for first just ahead of the Northern dialect. This indicates that Louisvillians place their own way of speaking between these two separate regional areas, giving preference to the Midwestern and Northern variet-ies, as might be expected from numerous other studies that have found stereotypical associations of correctness with these regions. Yet, Louisvil-lians acknowledge that their own variety is not quite as correct as those,

TABLE 4.8
Overall Rankings of Regions in Larger Regional Study

	Correct	Pleasant	Standard	Formal	Beautiful	Educated
Appalachia	11	5	10	10	7	10
Cajun/Creole	9	8	11	8	1	7
Chicago	1	4	2	3	6	4
Georgia	9	10	9	9	11	8
Kentucky	7	7	5	11	10	9
Louisville/Lexington	4	2	1	1	5	3
Mid-Atlantic	6	5	7	5	1	5
Midwest	1	3	2	3	1	2
Northern	3	8	4	2	9	1
Southern	5	1	8	6	1	6
Tennessee	8	11	6	7	8	11

further indicating that Louisville speech is slightly more correct than a broad Southern region. Appalachia was rated last in this category, which, as discussed above, partially serves to distance Louisvillians from the negative stereotypes they believe to be associated with that region.

Even though they do not feel confident enough to rate their variety as high in correctness as the Midwestern and Northern varieties, they do regard the Louisville/Lexington dialect as rather pleasant. Yet again, however, the ranking for this area falls between two regional delimitations, this time between Southern and Midwestern dialects, where Southern dialects get the highest designation. Again, the rating of the South as most pleasant is not surprising, given both the results of numerous language attitude studies and the larger national discourse about "Southern hospitality." The notion of Louisville as a place between places is evoked again.

In addition to the typical correctness/pleasantness ratings of perceptual dialectology, my research examines other social characteristics of language. Because the notion of "standard" language is so pervasive in discussions of American English, it seemed important to also explore how Louisvillians situate their own city in this dimension. Interestingly, they rate the Louisville/Lexington variety as most standard. This result, in combination with the two previous ones, suggests that the level of linguistic security among Louisvillians is unclear. The high ratings for standardness and pleasantness for Louisville/Lexington could indicate a high level of linguistic security, on par with that of Preston's (1989) Michigan sample. Yet the mediocre rating given to Louisville/Lexington in terms of correctness indicates this level of linguistic security might not be so high, perhaps more like Preston's (1989) southern Indiana respondents.[4] Louisvillians make some distinction between correctness and standardness; their variety is considered standard, but not necessarily correct.

As with standardness, Louisvillians believe their own variety to be the most formal one. It is also in this category that we see the most separation between how Louisvillians perceive their city's variety and how they perceive the larger state variety, which was rated as least formal. This massive difference in formality between the speech of Louisville/Lexington and Kentucky is somewhat surprising, given that both dialects were not considered to be statistically significantly different in the degree of difference task. It suggests a distancing among Louisvillians between their variety and the variety in the rest of the state, which is achieved by claiming a difference in level of formality. The differences between these two dialects have not been this great in the other social categories; perhaps level of formality is the factor which distinguishes urban and rural varieties for Louisvillians, which would explain the drastic distinction. Additional support for this division comes from the fact that Appalachia was also rated very low in this category (just ahead of Kentucky), further suggesting an urban/rural/ mountain rural divide (see Cramer 2016). Thus, just as in many other parts of the world (e.g., work being done by the SLICE group in Europe and elsewhere; see Sandøy 2011), urban varieties are typically connected with certain types of prestige that are simply not available to rural ones.

Despite there being no statistically significant results in the category of beauty, we can consider what the ranking says about how Louisvillians perceive their own variety. Kentucky appears again near the bottom of the rankings, just above Georgia. The Louisville/Lexington dialect is ranked fifth, though with a four-way tie for first, that ultimately means they classified it in second place. But this ranking near the middle of the group suggests again that Louisvillians may not be completely linguistically secure. Two of the regional dialects Louisvillians had placed their own variety between in other social categories (Midwest and Southern) are now both ranked higher than Louisville/Lexington, while the Northern variety is ranked near the bottom. So it appears in the case of beauty, Louisvillians do not classify themselves as highly as Midwest or Southern varieties, but by giving low ratings to those varieties that they perceive to be ugly varieties like the Georgia, Kentucky, and Northern dialects, they still essentially separate their own variety from them in that respect.

Turning to the question of education, we see that Louisvillians rated the Louisville/Lexington dialect as third most educated, echoing the results of the level of correctness analysis above. This appears to be a theme, wherein Louisvillians make a concerted effort to separate themselves from certain stigmatized stereotypes of the South (and Appalachia), like the stereotype of the uneducated Southerner being exposed here. Participants again clearly make some distinction between the Louisville/Lexington dialect and the Kentucky one, as they yet again separated these varieties in their rankings by a fairly large margin. This perhaps points again to the rural/urban divide within the state, with Louisvillians choosing to support the stereotype of educated city-dwellers versus uneducated rural residents.

In addition to the quantitative language attitudes questions participants answered on the surveys that accompanied the map drawing activities, data were also provided in the form of responses to open-ended questions. These questions addressed the other ways in which participants might describe a particular way of speaking, the reasons behind a participant's selection of a particular label for this way of speaking, and the meaning behind the label that was selected by the participant. We can explore these data for the regional map task to find the patterns among the Louisville participants in describing the regions they have delimited in open response form.

TABLE 4.9
Summary of Content Analysis of Stance toward Varieties

	Labels	Open-Ended Responses
Positive	4	32
Neutral	58	190
Negative	32	40
TOTAL	94	262

A content analysis of the labels used and the answers to the open-ended questions reveals some of these patterns. For each label and response, I coded whether the participant indicated a positive, neutral, or negative stance toward that which had been written. A summary of that analysis can be seen in table 4.9. This table shows that the responses, though overwhelmingly neutral, featured many instances where participants took a negative stance toward the varieties they delimited, and the negative stance slightly outnumbers the instances of positive stance.

In the open-ended questions, one rather common theme in the responses seemed to be a justification of position, typically as a way of demonstrating cultural sensitivity. For instance, one person wrote for four different labels that the label was "only perception—not reality," indicating that she knew that the label was stereotypical and not necessarily representative of the group being designated. Another respondent, in describing the Mid-Atlantic region, claimed that it was "a pattern of speech that, although a little different from my own is still as valid in its own way," a qualification he repeated for other labels.

This pattern is verified in a content analysis of the open-ended responses. In this case, open-ended questions were coded as expressing cultural sensitivity if punctuation was used to indicate separation from a given label or word choice (Cramer 2015a), if the response included both positive and negative attributes (wherein the positive one appears after the negative one as a way of mitigating the negative), if mitigating adverb or adjectives like "somewhat" or "slightly" appear with negative attributes, or if they explicitly use the word "stereotype" or in some way expressed that they did not mean the label/answer in a derogatory way. In total, 46 responses to the open-ended questions (out of 262 answers given) were coded as having some level of mitigation.

As suggested above, some participants overtly mentioned the word "stereotype" (only five instances of the word), so as to protect themselves from being associated with such ideas. One participant claimed that the rural Kentucky dialect she had designated was "stereotyped uneducated."

Another person admitted that the reason she selected a particular label for the Tennessee region had to do with "travel experience, stereotypes." One participant suggested that she selected the label "Southern Drawl" for the Southern region because of "past descriptions/stereotypical?" I am unsure as to the intended meaning of the question mark, but this same formation is used by another participant, who claims to have selected the label "Hillbilly" for the Appalachia region because it is a "Stereotypical term, perhaps, that I've heard before?"

Others chose different routes to avoid being thought of as culturally insensitive. In describing Appalachia, one respondent suggested that while speakers there are "[r]esistant to standard american english [...] locals are proud of their distinct ways of speaking." Others tried to soften the blow by using additional, lessening adjectives, as in "somewhat redneck" to describe Georgia and "Innocently simple" to describe Kentucky. One participant described Southern speech as possibly "grating or beautiful, depending on who's speaking," which suggests that the identity of the interlocutor is more important than the dialect he or she uses. Another description of the Southern region labels the variety as "Casual, but friendly," neither of which seem negative, but the inclusion of this conjunction that implies opposition indicates the participant believes she may have made a negative statement.

Some participants, however, did not hold back in their descriptions, providing further negative detail in the open-ended responses. These responses are included in the 40 that were categorized as negative in table 4.9. One respondent described the speech of Tennessee as sounding like "a 'clothespin' on the nose." The speech of the Northern region was described as "Short to the point. Northern unhospitality," "choppy," "possibly snippy," "cold, unfriendly, rushed," "stand offish," "rude," "high-pitched accent, annoying," "stuffy," "condescending," and "almost an attitude of not wanting to be bothered with." The speech of the Appalachia region was described as "hard to understand," "red-neck," "poor grammar...sometimes monotone," "hayseed/backwards," "isolated," "comical," and "uneducated."

In addition to simply listing adjectives associated with varieties of English, some participants chose to list the linguistic features they associated with the dialect. In the individual labels participants used, 35 of the 94 mentioned something to do with language (i.e., used the word "accent," described a linguistic phenomenon, indicated something to do with understanding and comprehension of the speech). In the open-ended responses, a large percentage of responses (88 out of 262 responses) mentioned something to do with language or linguistic features. This is perhaps not surprising, given the context in which the data were collected, but the number of responses referring to language outnumbered those referring simply to geography (another likely response in the context of this study). Only geography outnumbers language in terms of content of responses, such that 116 of 262 responses mention some aspect related to the geographical location of the variety under discussion. In terms of labels, a majority of the responses (71 out of 94) made some reference to geographic location.

Participants noted a sing-song style about the Appalachia region, such that one suggested it "sometimes also sounds like a song...a 'sawng'." Another participant claimed that "It seems when I am in Eastern Ky in the mountains the folks have the same rhythm or cadence in their speech." Such depictions of the rhythmic style of speech in Appalachia have been discussed elsewhere (e.g., Williams 1992).

In discussing the language of Chicago, one participant noted the speed or fast pace of the speech there. In contrast, the speech of Georgia is described as being "Slow, like it is so much fun that it's worth drawing out." It is suggested that the speech of Kentucky features "Drawn out words," while Northern speakers are "Short to the point." Southern speech is also frequently described as slow and drawn out.

Many participants focused on the phonetics of a region. One participant pointed to the well-known way in which Chicagoans pronounce the name of their city, with the "pronunciation of ah sound—Distinct way of saying Chicahgo, Wiscahnsin, etc. pahp." A well-known feature of Southern speech, the monophthongization of /aɪ/, is mentioned by two participants, one who claims that the speech is "Slow, long i sound specifically marks sound quality." The same feature is indicated in the speech of Tennessee, which is also described as drawn out and nasal.

From these adjectives and explicit commentary on the language spoken in certain areas in the regional dialect landscape, we get a better sense of the overall interpretation Louisvillians have of particular areas. If we consider the Midwest, we see that there is a strong focus on how the Midwest is perceived as being representative of Standard American English. More often than other varieties, the Midwestern dialect is referred to as "neutral," "standard," or "correct," with at least one participant indicating that it is how they "expect news anchors to sound." For other participants, Midwest speech is best represented in the speech of farmers. In addition to geography and the fact that "sound qualities make it distinct," one participant noted that he selected the label "Midwestern" because "it is related to the general cultural lifestyle of that area." In general, the impression one gets about the Midwest from the perspective of Louisvillians is that they highly value the speech there. In particular, they seem to value what they perceive to be standard speech spoken in the Midwest.

The Southern region is also described in mostly pleasant ways. Southerners and their speech are seen as "down to earth, relaxed," "lilting," "friendly, melodic," "layedback," "calm," "happy," "hospitable," "comfortable," and "refined." One participant even mentioned that a "Deep southern accent" makes her "think of sweet tea and porch swings, calm." Another noted that, "The people seem to not let anything bother them." Again, Louisvillians seem to value this way of speaking. In particular, the fascination seems to be with the positive Southern stereotypes of warmth and hospitality. The fact that Louisvillians seem to value both the Midwest and Southern regions, though in different ways, suggests, as we saw in the quantitative language attitudes data, that Louisvillians sometimes want to be considered both, but only if they are perceived as having only the positive features associated with each region.

So, what do Louisvillians say about Louisville specifically? The border mentality is made clearer through the comments provided in this section. One participant claimed that he might also describe the speech of Louisville as "a blend of Northern (Indiana) and Southern Ky speech." Another indicated that the speech in Louisville is "not as slow as southern dialect but not as fast as midwest," adding further that "it has the inbetween qualities." This participant also claimed that the speech found in Louisville is representative of "people who live along the mason-dixon line." Thus, at least some of these participants understand Louisville to be situated at some important border, one that makes it distinct from the regions that are located nearby.

These results reveal some interesting facts about Louisvillians and their understanding of Louisville's regional location. One clear pattern is a distancing from all that is considered bad. Louisvillians do not want to classify their own dialect alongside the uneducated, incorrect, nonstandard varieties that are stereotypically thought to be found in the Southern United States, but they also do not want to be associated with the Northern rudeness so many were quick to address. This "best-of-both-worlds" approach hints to their resistance to classification. Louisvillians believe that they can be both "a little of this and a little of that, and not quite one or the other" (Rosaldo 1993, 209) without having to be pigeon-holed into one category. This mentality comes from their recognition of their place on the border between these multiple places. The fact that they rank themselves high in pleasantness and correctness, for instance, shows that, unlike the typical Southerner who has been plagued by linguistic subordination, Louisvillians have a certain level of linguistic security that allows them to take pride in their way of speaking. Yet, they still subordinate their speech to the Midwest and Northern varieties in that sometimes, as in level of education, in that

Louisvillians rate these varieties ahead of their own. This unclear position in terms of linguistic security is indicative of the effect the border has on Louisvillians' perceptions of regional variation in the United States.

Additionally, as we have seen, Louisvillians take great strides to distance themselves not just from the South in general, but also from Kentucky and Appalachia in particular. Louisvillians are aware of the stereotypes people have of Kentuckians/Appalachians: they do not wear shoes, they marry their cousins,[5] and they do not value education. Thus, because Louisville is located in Kentucky (as is part of Appalachia) and is thereby commonly associated with these stereotypes, Louisvillians seek a way to widen the gap between their own way of speaking and how the rest of the state speaks. Thus, Kentucky becomes the scapegoat, as it were, for all that is considered wrong within the South.

If Kentucky is the scapegoat, how do Louisvillians differentiate themselves when the discussion moves from regional to statewide variation? A summary of the language attitudes rankings presented in chapter 3 for the Kentucky map project is presented in table 4.10. As we will see, Louisvillians use similar tactics in their attitudes about varieties within the state in establishing an identity for their own city.[6]

As noted in chapter 3, Eastern Kentucky is rated lowest in all social categories. This is similar to how the Appalachia region was described in the larger regional study. Conversely, Central Kentucky/Bluegrass (where Louisville is positioned) and Northern Kentucky are always rated highest. In fact, only in the case of formality was the Central Kentucky/Bluegrass region not rated best by Louisvillians. As was discussed above, Louisvillians place their own city in Central Kentucky, thus indicating that Louisvillians have a particularly high level of pride in the way that they speak as compared to other varieties in the state.

TABLE 4.10

Rankings of the Kentucky-Only Regions by Louisvillians and Kentuckians

	Correct		Pleasant		Standard		Formal		Beautiful		Educated	
	Lou	Ky	Lou	Ky	Lou	Ky	Lou	Ky	Lou	Ky	Lou	Ky
Central Ky./Bluegrass	1	2	1	1	1	2	2	2	1	1	1	2
Eastern Kentucky	5	5	5	5	5	5	5	5	5	5	5	5
Northern Kentucky	2	1	2	2	2	1	1	1	2	3	2	1
Southern Kentucky	3	4	4	4	3	4	4	4	3	4	3	4
Western Kentucky	4	3	3	3	3	3	3	3	3	2	4	3

Again, these ratings can be attributed to Louisvillians choosing to distance themselves from the negative stereotypes that are commonly applied to their state. In the larger national discourse about Kentucky, the state name is often seen as synonymous with the Appalachian region (Harkins 2015), which is typically associated with numerous negative stereotypes, like poverty, violence, and general backwardness (see Billings, Norman, and Ledford 1999). As such, Louisvillians feel a need to separate themselves from such stereotypes. They do so by rating Eastern Kentucky as low as possible in these language attitude surveys and by placing Louisville's region on the other end of the spectrum.

Appalachia is further marked as different by the use of certain derogatory labels and sentiments by participants when discussing the Eastern Kentucky region. Many participants used labels like "inbred," "hillbilly," "backwards," "poor," "redneck," "hick," and "country bumpkin" to describe the region, its language, and its people. Within the Kentucky data as a whole, many non-Appalachians described the language as hard to understand and lacking grammar. Louisvillians also described the people as uneducated, ignorant, stupid, and lazy, further indicating their acceptance of the negative stereotypes and their need to distinguish themselves from the region they perceive to possess these negative characteristics.

This differentiation is also accomplished by classifying Louisville as a Central Kentucky/Bluegrass variety, which was rated very highly in the surveys. The higher ratings for this region and for Northern Kentucky can be attributed to their association with urban areas. Fridland and Bartlett (2006) suggest that larger cities are often associated with prestige, which results in these areas having higher rankings. Louisvillians see their own city as worthy of such prestige, giving the region that encompasses the city the highest ratings in almost all categories.

In the descriptions of Northern and Central Kentucky, Louisville participants used labels like "standard," "appropriate," "normal," "proper," and "neutral." Additionally, many made references to Ohio, the Northern United States, and cities as a way of marking these regions as different than others in the state. One of the most common ways in which Louisvillians marked a difference between these urban areas and the rest of the state was through the juxtaposition of neutral, geographic labels like "central" for the Louisville area with negative labels for others, like "hillbilly" for Eastern Kentucky. One participant even relied on implicature by using "literate" to describe Central Kentucky, implicating that other varieties in the state are not. While most descriptions tended to be positive for Central and Northern Kentucky, words like "slang" or "uppity" could occasionally be found.

Louisvillians perceive linguistic divisions in the state that are best categorized as representing an urban/rural/mountain rural trichotomy (see also Cramer 2016). It is this division, one that coincides well with broader cultural impressions and stereotypes in the American dialect landscape, that showcases how Louisvillians utilize a "best-of-both-worlds" approach, especially when considered in combination with the results of the larger regional study. They want to align their way of speaking with every possibly positive attribute, as best they can, and disalign with negative ones. The Kentucky study shows that while they relegate their variety to a lower place in the larger region, they are very linguistically secure in their position within the state.

4.4. DISCUSSION

In examining the folk perceptions Louisvillians have about Louisville's place in the dialect landscape of the region and state, the findings show that Louisvillians categorize their city in a few ways: (1) often, the city is given no regional or state designation, indicating either that participants do not see their way of speaking as particular or that they see it as neutral, and therefore unworthy of comment; (2) the city can be considered its own separate variety, as indicated by the overarching category label Louisville/Lexington in the larger regional study and by the many individual maps that chose Louisville as its own region; (3) the city, at least in the regional study, is sometimes positioned at a border of two dialect regions, such that Louisville can be considered both Midwestern and Southern in the larger regional dialect landscape; and (4) within the Kentucky study, Louisville exists as an urban island in the largely (mountain) rural state.

In these tasks, Louisvillians placed their own variety in opposition to other areas, and in providing the data analyzed here, they show exactly how they understand Louisville's belonging. Thus, while the tendency may be for Louisvillians to associate their way of speaking with that of the Midwest or that of urban areas, their rating of their variety such that it is in line with the positive stereotypes associated with both the North and the South suggest that Louisvillians opt for the "best-of-both-worlds" approach in classifying their own way of speaking. In the next chapter, we turn our attention to non-Louisvillians and their ways of classifying the Louisville way of speaking. As we will see, the impression non-Louisvillians have of Louisville is rather different than Louisvillians have of themselves.

5. THROUGH SOMEONE ELSE'S EYES

IDENTITY IS NOT SIMPLY about how one sees oneself. From a sociocultural perspective, identities are conceived of as socially constructed (Bucholtz and Hall 2004) and are assumed to be dynamic (Bucholtz 1999). As has been shown in previous chapters, "[i]dentity is the social positioning of the self and other" (Bucholtz and Hall 2005, 586), such that Louisvillians are able to define themselves by not only asserting similarities with some group, but also by differentiating themselves from others. Therefore, in order to have a complete view of the regional identity of Louisvillians, we also have to examine how people from outside the community view the citizens of Louisville in terms of their linguistic identities. This chapter explores similar data as previous chapters, but the respondents are non-Louisvillians from Kentucky.[1] In the analysis, I show not only how Louisville is characterized by non-Louisvillians, but also how non-Louisvillians distinguish themselves within the broader national dialect landscape and within the state.

5.1. A DIFFERENT IMAGE OF THE DIALECT LANDSCAPE

We begin by examining online survey data that exhibits how 33 non-Louisvillians characterize individual states, New York City, and Washington, D.C. in terms of correctness, pleasantness, and degree of difference. The map in figure 5.1 shows the ratings of non-Louisvillians for level of correctness. Non-Louisvillians rated Louisiana as the least correct state, with an average score of about 4.8, and Illinois as the most correct, with an average score of about 5.9. If we compare this map to the one displaying the results from Louisvillians (figure 3.1), we see that non-Louisvillians have a more positive view of the South as a whole for level of correctness, rating fewer states in the lowest category. They also, however, connect the notion of correctness more strongly to the Midwestern states than Louisvillians do. These two findings seem to suggest that non-Louisvillians feel a stronger tie to these Southern states, choosing to align more closely with them, while also more clearly exhibiting belief in the stereotype of the standard-speaking Midwesterner. Both groups have a similar positive view of Washington and Ohio and a similar negative view of Louisiana, Mississippi, and New Jersey. As it concerns the state of Kentucky, Louisvillians rate the state slightly higher in level of correctness than non-Louisvillians, which seems indicative of a lower level of linguistic security among non-Louisvillians.

FIGURE 5.1
Non-Louisvillians' Correctness Ratings

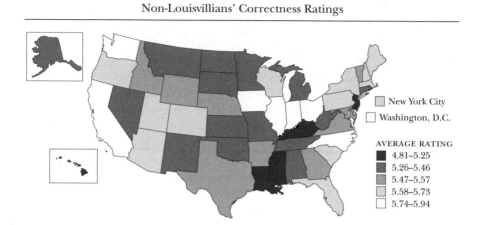

Next, in figure 5.2, the ratings for level of pleasantness for these non-Louisvillians are presented. Non-Louisvillians, like Louisvillians, rate New Jersey as the least pleasant variety, with an average score of about 5.70. Unlike Louisvillians, however, non-Louisvillians rate Kentucky as the most pleasant, with a score of 7.75. Again, this map can be compared to the map that was produced based on the Louisvillians' ratings (figure 3.2), in which case it appears that non-Louisvillians have a stronger negative view of the Southwestern and upper Midwestern states, rating more of them in the lowest category in pleasantness. As Kentucky was not rated as the most pleasant state for Louisvillians, we can say that non-Louisvillians have a more positive outlook on the state in this regard. They also have a less negative view

FIGURE 5.2
Non-Louisvillians' Pleasantness Ratings

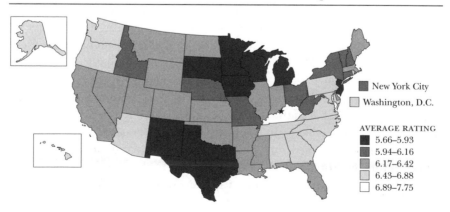

of Tennessee. Moreover, non-Louisvillians present a more broadly pleasant Southern region than Louisvillians, again showing a stronger allegiance to that region.

Interestingly, despite the differences found in terms of level of correctness and pleasantness, which revealed a tendency among non-Louisvillians to align with Southern states, the picture of variation in terms of degree of difference is very similar between the two groups. The map in figure 5.3, which can be compared to a similar map for the Louisville data (cf. figure 4.15), shows that non-Louisvillians also rate Indiana, Ohio, and Kentucky as least different from their own way of speaking. Louisvillians selected Indiana as the most similar, likely indicating geographic bias, while non-Louisvillians selected Ohio as most similar, with an average score of about 1.67. Both groups also agreed that Louisiana was most different, with non-Louisvillians rating the state at about 2.90. Finally, the picture of variation both in the Northeastern states and in the West look very similar between the two groups. It would appear, then, that both Louisvillians and non-Louisvillians align their ways of speaking more solidly with Midwestern varieties in terms of degree of difference.

The similarities between these two groups can also be found in some of the ways in which the dialect landscape of Kentucky is presented in the mental maps of non-Louisvillians in the state-only map drawing task. For example, the map in figure 5.4 represents a non-Louisvillian's mental map that follows the tendency of all Kentuckian maps to divide the state into four or five regions, using geographic or directional labels to name those areas. As in many other such maps, Louisville is situated in the Central Kentucky/Bluegrass region, as indicated by the location of the star.

FIGURE 5.3
Non-Louisvillians' Degree of Difference Ratings

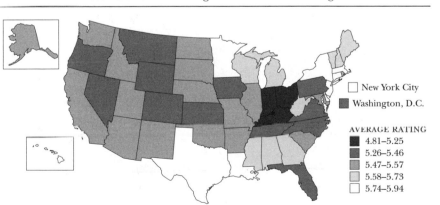

New York City
Washington, D.C.

AVERAGE RATING
4.81–5.25
5.26–5.46
5.47–5.57
5.58–5.73
5.74–5.94

FIGURE 5.4

Dialect Regions Drawn by a 22-Year-Old White Male from Edgewood, Kentucky

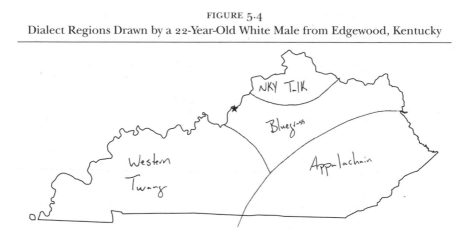

But there are also many ways that non-Louisvillians map variation in the state that differ from those of Louisvillians. For example, no Louisvillian produced an east-west divide like that in figure 5.5. This participant, who is from an area to the South of Louisville, distinguishes between the variety spoken in the eastern portion of the state, one that she perceives to consist of "Incorrect grammer," and the rest of the state, where a person "Talks Normal." It is surprising that no Louisvillians made this distinction, as the Appalachian region seemed to be the main area in the state from which participants tried to dissociate. Nonetheless, for this participant, the most important distinction in variation in the state is in correctness, and

FIGURE 5.5

Dialect Regions Drawn by a 30-Year-Old White Female from Bardstown, Kentucky

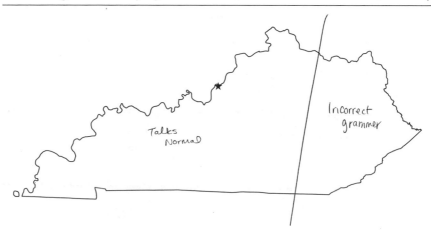

it coincides with an east-west divide that separates Appalachian Kentucky from the rest.

The previous map was, however, drawn by a person from an area that is, while certainly separate, located rather close to Louisville. The view from other Kentuckians in areas further from the city reveal other images. In figure 5.6, the participant has drawn three regions: a "Central Kentucky" region, which is perceived to be "proper" because of the colleges; a "Northern Kentucky" region, in which people speak like Ohioans; and an "Appalachian Region," where people talk in a way that the participant perceives as similar to her own speech. The presence of the third region is unsurprising, as the participant is from an Appalachian county. While Louisville is technically left uncategorized, the Central Kentucky region was likely meant to encompass the city, as references to colleges in the state usually refer to the University of Kentucky in Lexington and the University of Louisville. And while the descriptions of Central and Northern Kentucky in this map are not negative, the participant has clearly aligned with the Appalachian region and differentiated herself from the other areas.

The view from Lexington also shows this kind of alignment, as seen in the "Like me!" region in figure 5.7. This region, which includes Lexington, is considered by this participant to be "normal," which suggests the participant believes other regions in the state to fall short of such a designation. This rather detailed map features six regions, including a distinction between eastern and southeastern Kentucky that was not typically found in participant maps. Of particular interest here is the presence of a region called "Midwestern," which includes much of the state's northern border,

FIGURE 5.6

Dialect Regions Drawn by a 21-Year-Old White Female from Morehead, Kentucky

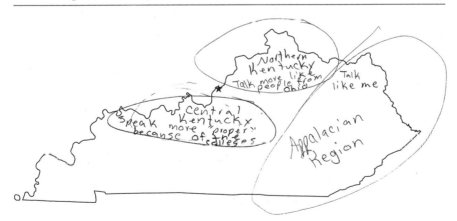

FIGURE 5.7

Dialect Regions Drawn by a 55-Year-Old White Female from Lexington, Kentucky

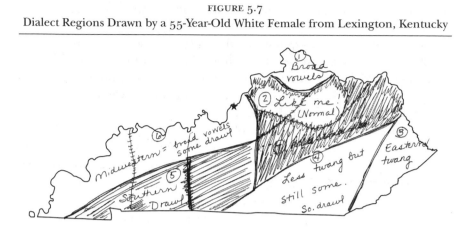

including Louisville and the remainder of the northern border to its west. Like the region located in the northernmost portion of the state, the "Midwestern" region is characterized by the presence of "broad vowels" but also features "some drawl," perhaps like the "Southern Drawl" region just to its south. Thus, like other categorizations of Louisville presented in this book, this Lexingtonian perceives the identity in this portion of the state to be mixed.

A view of the entire state presented by a participant from the western portion of the state in figure 5.8 is perhaps a little more negative. The labels "Ghetto," "Redneck," and "Country," while they could be construed more

FIGURE 5.8

Dialect Regions Drawn by a 24-Year-Old White Female
from Bowling Green, Kentucky

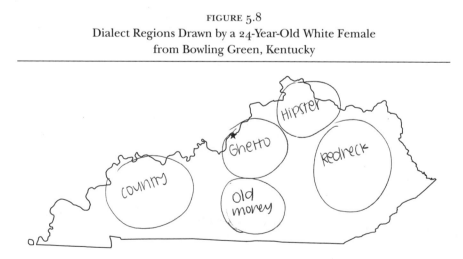

neutrally or even positively, are likely being used in a derogatory way, as evidenced by her very low attitudes ratings for those regions. The other two regions, "Old money" and "Hipster," receive higher ratings, with the former being classified as "classy" and "proper" and the latter being "modern" and "mainstream." Interestingly, she appears to connect the speech of her immediate area to this "Old money" region, thus providing a mostly positive take on the variety she perceives in her own community. This kind of pride in one's own speech community (also seen in figure 5.6 and figure 5.7 in the explicit aligning with certain regions) seemed more prevalent among non-Louisvillians than among Louisvillians.[2]

This positive spin on one's own community happened regularly with participants from Northern Kentucky. In these positive assessments, many Northern Kentuckians also disparaged other varieties in the state, especially ones spoken in the Louisville area. The map in figure 5.9 was drawn by a participant from one of the three counties in the northernmost portion of the state, in an area that is considered part of the larger Cincinnati, Ohio, metropolitan area (U.S. Census Bureau 2013). This participant has circled the area near his hometown and classified it as "Proper, educated Kentuckian," again suggesting that other areas in the state miss the mark for properness and educatedness. This suggestion is furthered by the circling of the

FIGURE 5.9

Dialect Regions Drawn by a 19-Year-Old White Male from Fort Thomas, Kentucky

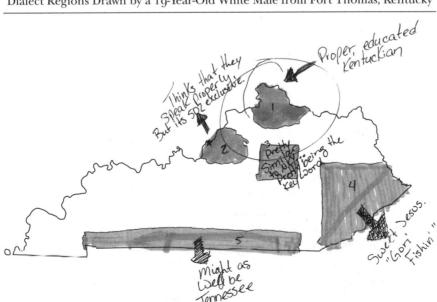

Louisville area with a claim that people "think" that they speak properly, indicating that the participant does not agree. Similarly, in the Lexington area, the participant claims that the speech there is similar to that which is spoken in Northern Kentucky, but he emphasizes that it is only similar, not exactly the same, by calling it "pretty similar" and by further indicating that "pretty" is "the key word." This participant also included an area along the Kentucky-Tennessee border, in the southern portion of the state, that he suggests "might as well be Tennessee" and another area, in the southeastern corner of the state, with the unclear label "Sweet Jesus. 'Gon' Fishin'.'"

In these maps, we see that the impressions non-Louisvillians have of the state can sometimes be similar to those of Louisvillians, but for the most part, they have slightly different views of the dialect landscape of the state. At the beginning of this section, we saw that these two groups also have varying views of the larger dialect landscape of the country, even though they agree on where speech is most similar. Thus, while non-Louisvillians seem to have stronger ties to the South in general, they also value Northern and Midwestern speech in ways that are similar to Louisvillians. The question remains, however, as to how non-Louisvillians understand Louisville's location in the dialect landscape of the state. In what follows, we examine how Louisvillians are explicitly characterized by non-Louisvillians, to explore the regional linguistic identities that non-Louisvillians attribute to the people from the largest city in their state.

5.2. DEPICTIONS OF LOUISVILLE

In general, when Kentuckians talk about Kentucky, one gets a sense that they do not feel that Louisville belongs. One might chalk this up to the large, in-state athletic rivalry between the University of Louisville, which has its major fan base in Louisville and its environs, and the University of Kentucky, which seems to have a fan base that includes the remainder of the state (and some in Louisville as well). Or perhaps it betrays the urban/ rural/mountain rural trichotomy we have seen presented elsewhere in this book. Regardless of the reason behind this distinction, the question remains as to whether there is evidence for such a distinction in the linguistic perceptions of non-Louisvillians.

To get a better sense of how Louisville fits in this non-Louisvillian image of the dialect landscape of Kentucky, we can consider other individually drawn mental maps (completed within the state-only map drawing task) of non-Louisvillians that specifically highlight Louisville's location. For example, the map in figure 5.10 shows some of this negative impression that we

FIGURE 5.10

Dialect Regions Drawn by a 32-Year-Old White Female from Pikeville, Kentucky

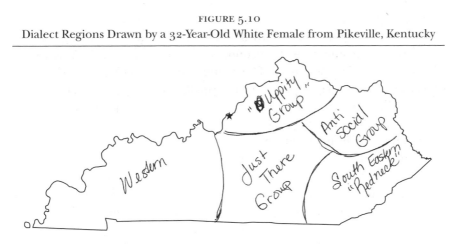

have seen in the previous section as well. This participant, from far eastern Kentucky, has grouped Louisville with Northern Kentucky under the label "'Uppity Group,'" a label that underlies the negative evaluation this participant gave of the region in the language attitudes survey that accompanied the map drawing task. To be fair, she appears to have a generally negative view of the state, using labels like "Anti Social Group," "Just There Group," and "South Eastern 'Redneck'" to describe a large portion of the state. Nonetheless, her understanding of linguistic variation in the state is such that Louisvillians' speech is perceived to be snobbish.

A similar perspective, from another participant from Eastern Kentucky, can be seen in figure 5.11. For this participant, there are only two varieties

FIGURE 5.11

Dialect Regions Drawn by a 38-Year-Old White Male from Prestonburg, Kentucky

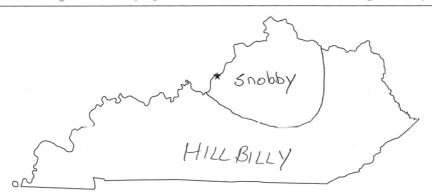

spoken in the state: "Snobby" and "HILLBILLY." Louisville is included in the "Snobby" region, along with northern Kentucky and Lexington, the three areas that compose the economic "Golden Triangle" of Kentucky (Tenkotte and Claypool 2009). The delineation, then, coincides with a view of Kentucky that is largely rural with a smaller urban portion, and in this case, neither region is given a very positive name. The participant claims the "HILLBILLY" variety is most similar to his own, but both regions are rated rather low in many attributes.

Not all visions of Louisville are bad, however. The participant who drew the map in figure 5.12 circled an area similar to the "Golden Triangle" discussed in chapter 4, which still encompasses Louisville but has now been labeled "High Class KY." Class and snobbery may be conceived of as two sides of the same coin, so it appears this participant has chosen the more positive reading. In all three cases, participants are attributing something to a Louisville way of speaking that differs from the rest of the state, and whether positive or negative, the association, based on the results of the language attitudes survey, has a great deal to do with Louisville being perceived a bastion of educated, correct, and standard speech, the combination of which results in the classy/snobby characteristic being invoked.

In many cases, as we saw in the previous chapter, Louisville was simply left unmarked by non-Louisvillians. Or, in stark contrast to Louisvillians' accuracy in pinpointing their city on the blank map, non-Louisvillians would frequently circle areas outside of the city with the clear intention of representing Louisville, as in figure 5.13. The area labeled "Cosmopoli-

FIGURE 5.12
Dialect Reagions Drawn by a 28-Year-Old White Female
from Bowling Green, Kentucky

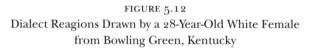
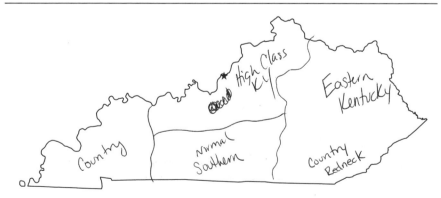

FIGURE 5.13

Dialect Regions Drawn by a 70-Year-Old White Female from Lebanon, Kentucky

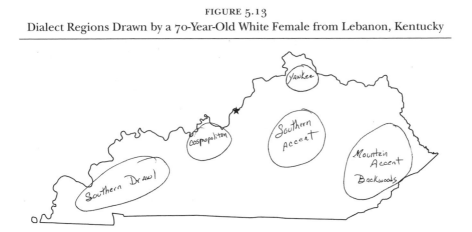

tan," a word often used to describe cities, is actually a bit downriver from Louisville in an area that includes a fifth-class city with a population around 2,000 (Brandenburg, Kentucky) as the largest town within the boundaries. It is likely that she intended to circle Louisville, as her answers to the open-ended questions in the language attitudes survey that accompanied the map drawing task indicated that people here were "city folks" and were from a "large city." I highly doubt the participant meant Brandenburg. I would argue that this misplacement of Louisville reveals more than geographic ignorance; the participant recognizes the existence of a Louisville variety but is unconcerned with its actual location because its existence plays little role in her own understanding of Kentucky's linguistic variation. It is there, wherever there is, but it is not important enough to need appropriate placement. Such an outlook reveals apathy toward Louisville, which seems to characterize several of the responses from non-Louisvillians in this data set (e.g., figure 5.6 above).

Another common phenomenon for non-Louisvillians was to connect the speech of Louisville to places outside of Kentucky. The participant who drew the map in figure 5.14, who happens to be originally from California but has spent the past four years living in Lexington for college, believes the speech of Louisville is most similar to that of (North) Nashville, Tennessee. This map is an anomaly, however, in that it was the only map to make a connection between Louisville and any specifically Southern locale. His delineation of Northern Kentucky as "South Cincy" reveals further that this participant perceives Kentucky as a whole to be a mix of the varieties spoken nearby, characterizing the state in a way similar to Louisvillians as

FIGURE 5.14

Dialect Regions Drawn by a 22-Year-Old White Male from California

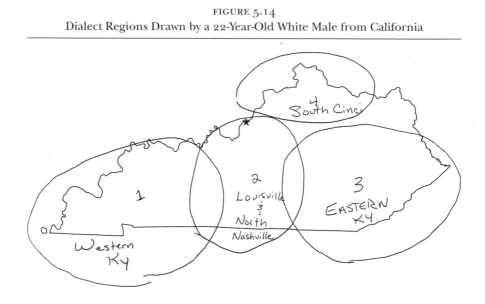

a middle ground between Midwestern places like Ohio and Southern ones like Tennessee.

Otherwise, the speech of Louisville was sometimes connected to a Midwestern state. The map in figure 5.15 is an example of one such connection, such that the speech of Louisville and that of Northern Kentucky is claimed to be "'Southern Cincinnati,'" a label very similar to the one found in figure 5.14. Unlike the previous map, however, the area of the state that can be connected to Tennessee is only that which borders that state, but the

FIGURE 5.15

Dialect Regions Drawn by a 51-Year-Old White Female from Lexington, Kentucky

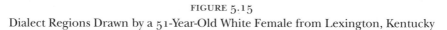

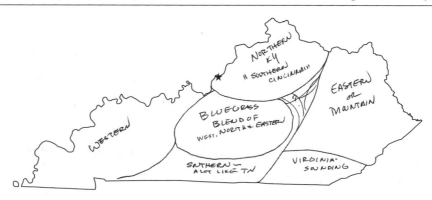

participant still indicates the mixed nature of speech in the state by choosing "Bluegrass Blend of West, North, and Eastern" for the variety in the central portion of the state. This blended region does not include Louisville, which suggests that this participant sees Louisville as being more squarely Midwestern (cf. figure 5.7 above).

Finally, and perhaps unsurprisingly, the Louisville way of speaking was also connected to an Indiana variety in figure 5.16. The sociocultural connections between Louisville and southern Indiana, which were explored in chapter 2, are quite strong, and their similarity in speech has also been presented elsewhere (e.g., José 2010). But this delimitation also might represent the mirror image of Preston's (1989) "frightened dissociation" expressed in the views of southern Indiana participants in his perceptual studies in communities on the other side of the Ohio River (see chapter 3). Whereas southern Indiana residents indicated a strong distinction between their own communities and those across the river in Kentucky in Preston's study (for fear of being associated with the negative stereotypes of Southernness they perceive there), this non-Louisville respondent wished to distance other Kentucky dialects, including his own, from the Louisville-Indiana speech located along the northern border of the state, perhaps for fear of having the rest of Kentucky be associated with perceived ills in Indiana. For this participant, those ills are the same as the ones discussed with regard to the first three maps in this section; namely, the participant claimed, in the open-ended questions on the language attitudes survey that accompanied

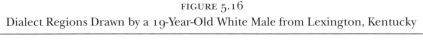

FIGURE 5.16
Dialect Regions Drawn by a 19-Year-Old White Male from Lexington, Kentucky

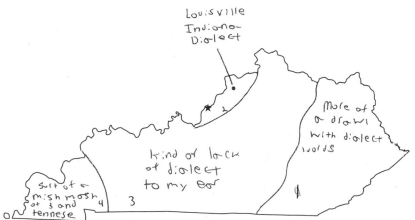

the map drawing task, that this variety was "pretentious and snobby with a hint of being stuck up," further indicating that this variety "stands out in KY most" as a "place that doesn't entirely belong to Kentucky."

One final map that can elucidate where Louisville belongs in the state can be seen in figure 5.17, which features the 50% agreement composite map for all Kentuckians.[3] Interestingly, if we compare this composite map to the composite map depicting only Louisville data (figure 3.24), the most striking difference is the central location of the Central Kentucky/Bluegrass region. For Louisvillians, the heart of this region is in Louisville. For Kentuckians as a whole, however, the center is situated more centrally in the state, closer to Frankfort, the state's capital and a more quintessentially Central Kentucky area in the larger discourse about the region.[4] This fact could be a relic of the fact that Louisville was classified as Central Kentucky in the analysis, and perhaps Louisvillians themselves were more likely than other Kentuckians to encircle a Louisville region as separate, thus pushing the center closer to the city. But an analysis that seems just as likely is that Louisville is just not as central in the minds of non-Louisvillians as it is for Louisvillians. Thus, like in figure 5.13, Louisville's location is simply not important for non-Louisvillians.

The picture that is painted of Louisville by non-Louisvillians seems to be somewhat different than the one Louisvillians paint of themselves. Non-Louisvillians perceive Louisville to be snobbish but cosmopolitan, to exist in the landscape but with an unimportant geographic position, and to represent places outside of Kentucky, or more explicitly, to not represent what they view as quintessential Kentuckianness. Therefore, the difference

FIGURE 5.17
Overall Composite Map of All Kentuckians' Responses with 50% Agreement

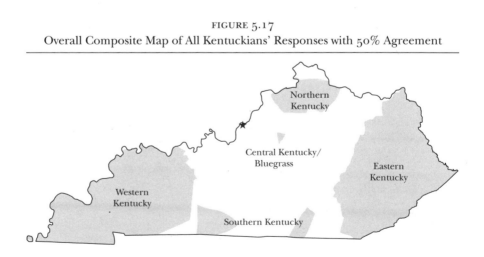

appears to be more than simply geographic. The attitudes that non-Louis-villians hold about Louisville also differ from how Louisvillians see themselves. In what follows, we explore these attitudes more carefully to better understand why non-Louisvillians have an apparent distaste (or disregard) for this large urban center. More specifically, we see the picture from that most stigmatized location within the state—Appalachia.

5.3. APPALACHIAN IMPRESSIONS

I turn again to the attitudes held by speakers as a way of understanding their notions of belonging. In this case, we can explore how non-Louisvillians rate Louisville and their own regions in terms of the social characteristics we have been exploring by returning to the language attitudes survey that accompanied the state-only map drawing task. Because Louisvillians have taken a particularly negative view of Eastern Kentucky, I limit my discussion here to the sentiments of Appalachians to see if there are any mechanisms by which Appalachians strike back at Louisvillians for such negative depictions.[5]

It comes as no surprise that Appalachians themselves view their own region in a negative way; the uptake of stereotypes directed at Appalachians by Appalachians is not new (see, e.g., Billings 1999). For example, in my Kentucky map data, a 19-year-old female from Floyd County labeled the eastern portion of the state "Redneck" because she is "from that area and highly embarrassed of it." Indeed, several Appalachian participants chose labels like "hick," "hillbilly," "redneck," and other words typically conceived of as derogatory to represent the Appalachian region.[6]

But Appalachians are not as hard on themselves as Louisvillians (or Kentuckians altogether) are. In table 5.1, we see the Appalachians' and Louisvillians' ratings for each of the social categorizations that appeared on

TABLE 5.1

Rankings of the Regions by Appalachians and Louisvillians

	Correct		Pleasant		Standard		Formal		Beautiful		Educated	
	App	Lou	App	Lou	App	Lou	App	Lou	App	Lou	App	Lou
Central Ky./Bluegrass	2	1	1	1	1	1	2	2	3	1	2	1
Eastern Kentucky	5	5	2	5	5	5	5	5	2	5	5	5
Northern Kentucky	1	2	5	2	2	2	1	1	5	2	1	2
Southern Kentucky	4	3	4	4	4	3	4	4	1	3	4	3
Western Kentucky	3	4	3	3	3	3	3	3	4	3	3	4

the language attitudes survey that accompanied the state-only map drawing activity. Unlike Louisvillians, Appalachians do not rate their own variety as worst in each category. They view their own speech as rather pleasant and beautiful, but they still subjugate their variety to others; in particular, Central Kentucky/Bluegrass is rated as most pleasant, and Southern Kentucky is rated as most beautiful. In addition to upgrading their own speech, they also downgrade that of others in the state. For example, Northern Kentucky was rated as least pleasant and least beautiful, though the results were not significant.

What do they think of Louisville? As noted previously, Louisville is most often categorized in the Central Kentucky/Bluegrass region. Thus, it appears that Appalachians generally view that dialect positively. It was rated as most pleasant and most standard, and it was rated second only to Northern Kentucky, the other region most likely to contain Louisville, in correctness, formality, and education.

The positivity, however, seems to stop there. Many labels used by non-Louisvillians to tag the Louisville region, as seen in the maps above, are words that are typically conceived of as derogatory like "Yankee," "Snobby," and "Ghetto." One Appalachian participant used the label "Urban Brogue" to describe the area including Louisville, further commenting that the variety spoken there was "snobbish, insulting, superior" and that the speakers of this variety "think they are better than everyone else," further highlighting the discussion in the previous section regarding the classy/snobby characteristic.

On the other hand, Appalachians' descriptions of their own variety were more positive, especially as contrasted with the ways in which Louisvillians described Appalachia. In describing their region, they typically made references and connections to their heritage, an approach not often exploited by Louisvillians in describing their own region. They also made more references to home and family when referring to Appalachia than Louisvillians did with Louisville.

These labels and sentiments, in connection with their language attitudes, reveals a pride in the local speech that is quite different than the picture painted of Appalachia by Louisvillians. And while Appalachians can be seen as striking back in the labels and sentiments they expressed about Louisville's region, the distaste for Central Kentucky/Bluegrass and Northern Kentucky is not enacted in their language attitudes. They still associate those regions with positive attributes like education and correctness. One might argue, then, that the vision of Louisville from the perspective of Appalachians is lukewarm; they find positivity in its association with education, especially as compared to their own variety, but they also see it as lacking very important qualities they associate with their own speech, like the importance of family and heritage. This difference mirrors the urban/rural/mountain rural distinction discussed previously, such that Appalachians use stereotypical notions of rurality, both positive (i.e., family values) and negative (i.e., lacking education), to differentiate themselves from the stereotypical social attributes of urbanity, again both positive (i.e., educated) and negative (e.g., disconnected from family ties), that they connect to Louisville.

5.4. DISCUSSION

In this chapter, we have encountered the view of the outsider. This encounter has revealed how non-Louisvillians see Louisville in terms of belonging in the dialect landscape of the state. We have also explored how non-Louisvillians distinguish themselves from Louisville through varying means. This chapter, perhaps more than any other, presents an image of the disputed place of Louisville. Whether it is in how non-Louisvillians differ from Louisvillians in their presentation of the national and state dialect landscapes or in how non-Louisvillians characterize Louisville in numerous ways as not belonging to the rest of the state, this image of Louisville's regional linguistic identity is clearly one that broadly contests any attachment to Southernness that Louisvillians might have expressed.

In the next chapter, we shift our attention away from perception and toward production. In examining production data taken from a reality television show set in Louisville, I demonstrate how the production of linguistic identity by Louisvillians is not straightforward either. I present an acoustic analysis of particular linguistic variables associated with Southern and Midwestern speech to depict the chaotic nature of regional linguistic identities in the city.

6. SOUTHERN LINGUISTIC FEATURES AND PRODUCTION OF IDENTITY

THIS CHAPTER INCLUDES an analysis of the vowel systems of five Louisville women (described in detail in chapter 1) in an examination of how regional identity is realized in the production of certain linguistic variables. Specifically, since dialect maps often position Louisville as part of the Southern dialect region, I explore the level of participation among these speakers in certain features associated with Southern speech, including the Southern Vowel Shift (SVS) (Fridland 1998, 2001; Labov, Ash, and Boberg 2006) and the front-lax prenasal merger (Bailey 1997; Labov 1996; Labov, Ash, and Boberg 2006; Thomas 2008), as well as in one feature that seems to be resisted in Southern speech, namely the low back vowel merger (Frazer 1996; Gordon 2006; Labov, Ash, and Boberg 2006; Irons 2007).

The SVS is a series of movements in the vowel space occurring in many dialects in the Southern United States. The phenomenon of /aɪ/-monophthongization is thought to be the catalyst for the shifts (e.g., Feagin 1986; Fridland 1998; Fridland 2000; Labov, Ash, and Boberg 2006), and this phenomenon, as well as the movement of vowels of the Front Shift (the inversion of /i/ and /ɪ/ and of /eɪ/ and /ɛ/) and the movement of vowels of the Back Shift (the fronting of /u/ and /oʊ/) are examined in this chapter.[1]

The front-lax pre-nasal merger (i.e., the PIN/PEN merger) refers to the merging of /ɪ/ with /ɛ/ before nasal consonants (hence, *pen* is produced such that it is homophonous with *pin*). The low back vowel merger (i.e., the COT/CAUGHT merger) refers to the merging of /ɔ/ with /ɑ/ in many phonetic contexts (such that *caught* is produced such that it is homophonous with *cot*).[2] These two mergers are thought to be complementarily distributed, such that Southern speakers tend to categorically exhibit the PIN/PEN merger but are resistant to the COT/CAUGHT merger (but see Bailey et al. 1993; Bowie 2000; Hazen 2005; Ash 2006; Gordon 2006; and Irons 2007 for instances of these mergers in locations outside of the expected regions of occurrence).

The data for this portion of the project come from an original SOAP-net reality television show, *Southern Belles: Louisville* (2009). More information about these data can be found in chapter 1. This chapter features an

acoustic analysis of the speech of each of the five main characters with reference to the linguistic variables mentioned above.[3]

Ultimately, this analysis of vowels reveals a great deal of variation in the
use of Southern and non-Southern dialectal features. Thus, as a comple-
ment to the analysis of the vowels themselves, I also examine the discursive contexts in which the most iconic Southern variant, /aɪ/-monophthon-
gization, appears in the data. The assumption is that these women, who
appear to have access to at least two linguistic systems, one that utilizes the
monophthongal variant and one that does not, can exhibit this variant as a
means to promote a Southern identity in context.

In summary, this chapter shows that the use or non-use of Southern
variants is rather chaotic, such that the purely numerical analysis reveals
widely varying usage patterns, including what appears to be a cline of participation in the shifts and exhibition of both mergers among the speakers.
The more subjective contextual analysis indicates that while Southern contexts might initiate use of the Southern variants, the choice in variant is not
so straightforward. In the following sections, I present both the quantitative
and qualitative analyses of the data and a discussion of those results.

6.1. ACOUSTIC ANALYSIS OF VOWELS

In this section, I present an acoustic analysis of the vowels involved in the
SVS, the PIN/PEN merger, and the COT/CAUGHT merger, as discussed above.
For the SVS, a total of ten tokens were randomly selected for each of the
vowel classes under investigation for each subject, for a total of 70 target
tokens per speaker. Additionally, tokens for two control vowels were also
collected. For the mergers, 10–14 tokens of each vowel were obtained for
each speaker, for a total of 40–56 target tokens per speaker. Vowels were
extracted from one syllable words in which the vowel was not word-initial.
For the PIN/PEN merger, vowel tokens preceded [n] and [m], while vowel
tokens for the analysis of the COT/CAUGHT merger preceded [t] and [k]
(Hazen 2005). For more information about these data, see chapter 1.

I examine each participant individually, as an overall analysis of five
women would likely not yield very interesting generalizations about Louisville as a whole. But the analysis of these individual women does provide
insight into the identity processes available for Louisvillians because of
their location at the border. Each subsection below discusses the findings
for each of the linguistic features under investigation and for each of the
participants in further detail. The participants are presented here in alphabetical order by first name.

6.1.1. MONOPHTHONGIZATION OF /aɪ/. The methodology used for analyzing /aɪ/-monophthongization in the *Southern Belles: Louisville* data comes from Cramer (2009), which, drawing on work by Thomas (2000), examined the steady-state patterns of the American English diphthong /aɪ/ for speakers in Louisville, Kentucky, as compared to Midland speakers from central Illinois. Within that study, one subject from the Southern dialect region was analyzed as a point of reference for the pattern exhibited in that region. Participants read a list of minimal pairs. Each word was monosyllabic and featured a consonant or consonant cluster, followed by /aɪ/, and ended with /t/ or /d/. The Midland and Southern patterns were established, and the Louisville data were compared to show whether Louisville speakers pattern with either one of these dialect groups.

In American English, diphthongs typically exhibit two steady-states: one in the onset, which is followed by a transition, and another in the offset (Lehiste and Peterson 1961). To analyze the speakers' use of the monophthongal variant, I exported the formant values from Praat for each token of /aɪ/ and, using MATLAB, applied an optimization-based curve fitting procedure to the F_1 and F_2 values. In this procedure, I was fitting the data to the ideal diphthong pattern using four parameters: transition beginning and end times and frequencies. Fitting to this pattern can allow for all other possible patterns to be described.[4]

The goal was to minimize the sum of the squares of errors using a piecewise linear regression model. The optimization procedure consisted of a linear least squares model nested in two line searches. A line search seeks to optimize a function of one variable on a line segment, in this case, attempting to minimize the curve-fitting error. The outer line search seeks the optimal transition beginning time by minimizing a function defined by a nested line search. This inner line search seeks the optimal transition end time (given a transition beginning time). Given the transition beginning and end times, it is possible to formulate an overconstrained linear equation in the beginning and end frequencies. Finding the least squares solution to the linear equation is a basic operation in MATLAB. The inner line search minimizes the error associated with the least squares solution. The type of line search used in this study is a Fibonacci line search, which iteratively narrows the range in which the optimal value must lie.[5] A vowel is declared monophthongal if the change in frequency (in F_1 or F_2) from the initial point of the vowel to the end point was less than 25%.[6]

In F_1, Emily used the monophthongal variant in four of ten cases. In F_2, she produced a monophthong in all but two words. All four cases where F_1 featured the monophthong also featured a monophthong in F_2, making these vowels complete monophthongs.[7] Table 6.1 features the individ-

TABLE 6.1
Level of Monophthong Use for Emily

Word	F_1		F_2	
	Z_2/Z_1	Monophthong?	Z_2/Z_1	Monophthong?
I	0.720361	FALSE	1.14424	TRUE
invited	0.737399	FALSE	1.452226	FALSE
I'm	1.063218	TRUE	1.110029	TRUE
time	1.13499	TRUE	0.857714	TRUE
kind	0.952238	TRUE	0.955882	TRUE
exciting	0.507763	FALSE	1.032022	TRUE
assignment	0.563025	FALSE	1.142991	TRUE
my	1.118502	TRUE	1.200418	TRUE
I've	0.604966	FALSE	0.74093	FALSE
decide	1.69919	FALSE	1.140123	TRUE

ual words, the ratios of the end frequencies to the beginning frequencies (Z_2/Z_1), and whether the ratio met the requirements of a monophthong as defined by the study, showing both F_1 and F_2 separately. The highlighted entries are complete monophthongs. Each table for the other four women is constructed in the same manner.

An example of a complete monophthong can be seen in Emily's production of the word *kind* (figure 6.1). The line, which indicates the best fit for the data points, clearly features only a small amount of transition in F_2

FIGURE 6.1
F_1 and F_2 for /aɪ/ in *kind* as Produced by Emily

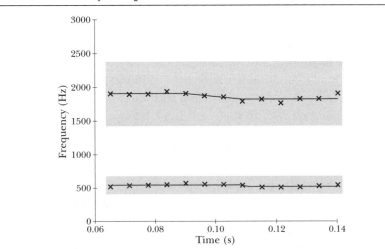

and seemingly no transition in F_1. My definition of a monophthong as consisting of at most a 25% change in frequency across the vowel is met in this vowel, and the graphical representation of this vowel shows rather plainly that this vowel is, in fact, a monophthong.

A statistical analysis of the data finds that Emily's use of monophthongs in F_2 is statistically significant, assuming a level of significance at $p < .05$, though her use in F_1 is not. I have also included 95% confidence intervals, which show that even though the interval for F_1 contains a probability of 50% of exhibiting a monophthong pattern at least as often as the Southern pattern, only the values in the interval for F_2 are almost entirely greater than 50%, with a lower bound quite close to 50%. The results are presented in table 6.2.

Information about Hadley's level of /aɪ/-monophthongization can be found in table 6.3. In F_1, Hadley used the monophthongal variant in three of ten words. In F_2, she produced a monophthong in seven of ten words. There were only two instances where both F_1 and F_2 were determined to be monophthongs.

TABLE 6.2
Statistical Analysis for Emily for /aɪ/

	F_1	F_2
p-value	0.431632	0.000326
Observed proportion	40%	80%
95% CI: lower bound	17%	49%
95% CI: upper bound	69%	94%

TABLE 6.3
Level of /aɪ/-Monophthongization for Hadley

	F_1		F_2	
Word	Z_2/Z_1	Monophthong?	Z_2/Z_1	Monophthong?
I	0.889346	TRUE	1.160482	TRUE
idea	0.659524	FALSE	1.220066	TRUE
I've	0.880338	TRUE	1.158072	TRUE
my	0.760456	TRUE	1.33141	FALSE
I'm	0.676849	FALSE	1.146317	TRUE
kind	0.474486	FALSE	0.90086	TRUE
I'll	0.664927	FALSE	0.724204	FALSE
finding	0.491478	FALSE	1.792759	FALSE
guys	1.704143	FALSE	0.951574	TRUE
guy	1.616764	FALSE	1.129567	TRUE

An example of a complete monophthong produced by Hadley can be seen in figure 6.2. This figure represents Hadley's production of the pronoun *I*. It is not unexpected that a common word like *I* might appear in the monophthongal form in a possibly marginally Southern accent because, as Feagin (2000, 342–43) notes, "the monophthongal unglided vowel in *I* and *my* symbolizes all Southerners' identification with the South." But as can be seen in table 6.3, Hadley uses the monophthongal variant in *I* and *I've*, a monophthong in F_2 of *I'm*, and no monophthong in *I'll*, so it cannot be generalized that Hadley always uses the monophthongal variant in variations of *I*. What the graphical representation shows again is that the vowel, perceived as a monophthong by the author, still has a slight amount of shift across the vowel, though not larger than the 25% criterion considered here.

The images of complete monophthongs alone might not show the entire picture. A comparison of figure 6.2 and figure 6.3, which is a representation of Hadley's production of the /aɪ/ in the word *finding*, shows how different the monophthongs appear relative to vowels that feature the typical diphthong pattern. Here, there is a large transition phase between two steady-states, which is lacking in figure 6.2. Also, F_1 and F_2 both start between 1,000 and 1,500 Hz, and while F_1 drops, F_2 increases, indicating the shift from the low, back /a/ to the high, front /ɪ/.

A statistical analysis of the data finds that Hadley's use of monophthongs in F_2 is statistically significant, assuming a level of significance at

FIGURE 6.2
F_1 and F_2 for /aɪ/ in *I* as Produced by Hadley

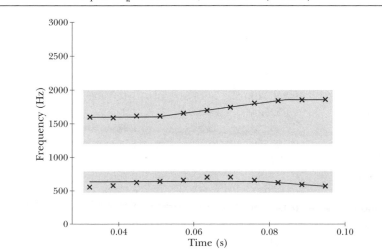

FIGURE 6.3

F_1 and F_2 for /aɪ/ in *finding* as Produced by Hadley

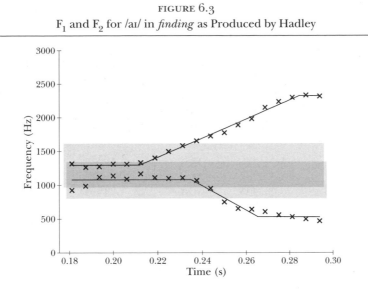

$p < .05$, though her use in F_1 is not. Again, while the intervals for both F_1 and F_2 contain a probability of 50% of exhibiting a monophthong pattern at least as often as the Southern pattern, more of the values for the interval for F_2 are above 50% rather than below it, while the majority of the range is located below 50% for F_1. The results are presented in table 6.4.

Table 6.5 shows Julie's level of /aɪ/-monophthongization. This table shows that there are four instances of monophthongs in F_1 and seven in F_2. There are three instances where both F_1 and F_2 were determined to be monophthongs.

An example of one of Julie's complete monophthongs can be seen in figure 6.4. Again, a slight transitional phase can be detected in both F_1 and F_2, but the amount of change in frequency across the vowel is less than 25%. Similar to Hadley's case, this figure represents Julie's production of *I'm*, which, like *I*, is likely to become monophthongal in a dialect that has

TABLE 6.4

Statistical Analysis for Hadley for /aɪ/

	F_1	F_2
p-value	0.692997	0.018549
Observed proportion	30%	70%
95% CI: lower bound	11%	40%
95% CI: upper bound	60%	89%

TABLE 6.5
Level of /aɪ/-Monophthongization for Julie

| Word | F_1 | | F_2 | |
	Z_2/Z_1	Monophthong?	Z_2/Z_1	Monophthong?
I	0.626654	FALSE	1.42316	FALSE
memorized	1.915488	FALSE	1.485803	FALSE
I'm	1.131347	TRUE	0.881645	TRUE
I'll	0.890328	TRUE	0.935806	TRUE
why	0.877389	TRUE	1.66882	FALSE
kinda	1.431471	FALSE	1.167569	TRUE
guys	1.326222	FALSE	0.940086	TRUE
sometimes	0.633463	FALSE	1.238234	TRUE
time	0.743768	FALSE	1.201671	TRUE
my	0.79565	TRUE	1.074404	TRUE

FIGURE 6.4
F_1 and F_2 for /aɪ/ in *I'm* as Produced by Julie

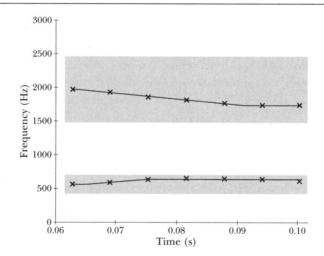

been influenced by Southern phonology. Additionally, Julie's production of *I'll* and *my* were the other two instances of complete monophthongs. However, figure 6.5 features the graphical image of Julie's production of *I*, which has the shape of a typical diphthong. Again, a generalization based on this information is not appropriate.

Kellie's overall level of /aɪ/-monophthongization can be seen in table 6.7. In F_1, the monophthong pattern is exhibited in four of the ten words. In F_2, all but two vowels were determined to be a monophthongal. Like Emily's, all four of Kellie's vowels where F_1 was determined to be a monoph-

FIGURE 6.5
F_1 and F_2 for /aɪ/ in *I* as Produced by Julie

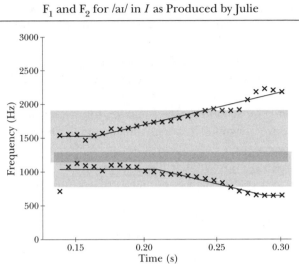

TABLE 6.6
Statistical Analysis for Julie for /aɪ/

	F_1	F_2
p-value	0.431632	0.018549
Observed proportion	40%	70%
95% CI: lower bound	17%	40%
95% CI: upper bound	69%	89%

TABLE 6.7
Level of /aɪ/-Monophthongization for Kellie

	F_1		F_2	
Word	Z_2/Z_1	*Monophthong?*	Z_2/Z_1	*Monophthong?*
I	0.806248	TRUE	0.935804	TRUE
kind	0.873164	TRUE	0.918893	TRUE
my	1.333607	FALSE	0.939343	TRUE
child	0.383851	FALSE	0.658798	FALSE
meantime	0.88388	TRUE	1.207033	TRUE
I'm	1.554371	FALSE	0.989759	TRUE
find	1.135358	TRUE	0.940683	TRUE
by	1.885134	FALSE	0.872578	TRUE
lifestyle	1.336664	FALSE	1.364695	FALSE
kinda	0.371074	FALSE	0.901266	TRUE

thong also featured a monophthong in F_2, making these vowels complete monophthongs. Kellie and Emily are tied for the most complete monophthongs, both with four instances where both F_1 and F_2 exhibit the monophthong pattern.

An example of one of Kellie's complete monophthong can be seen in figure 6.6. As with Hadley and Julie, an example of *I* from Kellie is revealed as a complete monophthong. One data point seems to be slightly out of place (at about 0.05 seconds), which causes the somewhat drastic transitional phase between two fairly straight steady-states. Despite this issue, the graphical representation exhibits a rather clear monophthongal pattern. Yet, as with the previous women, while this instance of *I* is a monophthong, table 6.7 indicates that Kellie's production of *my* and *I'm* only featured a monophthong in F_2.

A statistical analysis of the data finds that Kellie's use of monophthongs is statistically significant only in F_2, assuming a level of significance at $p < .05$. The intervals for both F_1 and F_2 contain a probability of exhibiting

FIGURE 6.6

F_1 and F_2 for /aɪ/ in *I* as Produced by Kellie

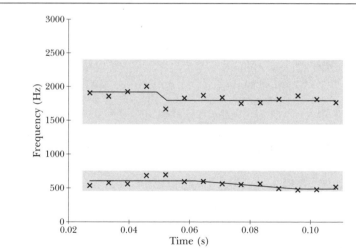

TABLE 6.8

Statistical Analysis for Kellie for /aɪ/

	F_1	F_2
p-value	0.431632	0.000326
Observed proportion	40%	80%
95% CI: lower bound	17%	49%
95% CI: upper bound	69%	94%

a monophthong pattern at least as often as the Southern pattern of greater than 50%, but again, the values are higher in F_2. The results are presented in table 6.8.

Shea's level of /aɪ/-monophthongization can be seen in table 6.9. In F_1, three of the curves produced were determined to be monophthongal. In F_2, eight out of ten were determined to be monophthongs. Two of the three monophthongal patterns in F_1 also aligned with monophthongs in F_2 for complete monophthongs.

An example of a complete monophthong can be seen in figure 6.7, which is a graphical representation of Shea's production of the word *decide.* Here, there is only a slight transition in both F_1 and F_2, both of which cause a change in frequency across the vowel of less than 25%.

A statistical analysis of the data finds that, like the others, Shea's use of monophthongs is statistically significant only in F_2, assuming a level of significance at $p < .05$. While the intervals for both F_1 and F_2 contain a probability of 50% of exhibiting a monophthong pattern at least as often as the Southern pattern, the values for the interval for F_2 are higher than those for F_1. The results are presented in table 6.10.

This section reveals the varying degrees to which these five women utilize the Southern feature of the monophthongal variant of /aɪ/. Emily and Kellie lead the way with the most instances of the monophthong in their speech (12 of the 20 total curves defined as monophthongs, counting F_1 and F_2 separately, and four complete monophthongs each). Julie and Shea were next, with 11 of 20 curves defined as monophthongs, and Hadley had the least amount, with 10 of 20 curves defined as monophthongs. That said, the total number of monophthongs for all of the women was at least

TABLE 6.9
Level of /aɪ/-Monophthongization for Shea

| Word | F_1 | | F_2 | |
	Z_2/Z_1	Monophthong?	Z_2/Z_1	Monophthong?
I've	1.032057	TRUE	0.880429	TRUE
decide	1.192914	TRUE	0.966586	TRUE
liner	0.953645	TRUE	1.417447	FALSE
I	2.059912	FALSE	0.900058	TRUE
kind	0.534898	FALSE	0.882047	TRUE
lives	1.691689	FALSE	1.158704	TRUE
time	0.678032	FALSE	1.05476	TRUE
I'm	0.706303	FALSE	1.018932	TRUE
my	0.672218	FALSE	1.315383	FALSE
find	0.613377	FALSE	1.052925	TRUE

FIGURE 6.7

F_1 and F_2 for /aɪ/ in *decide* as Produced by Shea

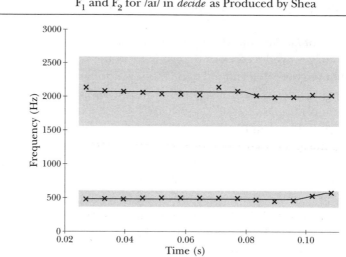

50%, a rather medial number for speakers representing a city in the South-ern dialect area, which is defined by its monophthongization of /aɪ/. In fact, the number echoes the result for Louisville in Labov, Ash, and Boberg's (2006) map. I argue that this figure provides more evidence to the fact that Louisville is on a border between a dialect that participates in the process of monophthongization of /aɪ/ and one that does not, making it just as likely that the speakers will produce either variant.

6.1.2. REVERSAL OF FRONT TENSE AND LAX VOWELS. Drawing heavily on the methodology presented in Fridland (1998, 2000, 2001), this sec-tion addresses the shift occurring in the front vowels of many Southern speakers. Using the means of the mid values of the vowel tokens of /eɪ/, /ɛ/, /i/, and /ɪ/, I compared the vowel space of each subject to that of an unshifted speaker (Peterson and Barney 1952). The vowel space of the female unshifted speaker that serves as the point of reference for this study can be seen in figure 6.8; the values used for plotting her vowel space are provided in table 6.11. The information for plotting the monophthongal vowels comes from Peterson and Barney, but values were not provided for diphthongs. The values for /eɪ/ and /oʊ/ were taken from Stevens (1998). While the measurements from Peterson and Barney certainly have limita-tions (see Hillenbrand et al. 1995; Labov 2010), it was deemed reasonable to compare these speakers to the unshifted female because it is the most commonly cited experiment of its type and the speech is said to represent "general American." Or, in the authors' own words, their "methods of mea-surement and analysis have been found to resolve the effects of different

FIGURE 6.8
Vowel System of an Unshifted Female
(Peterson and Barney 1952)

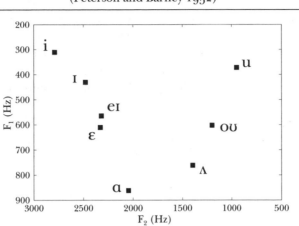

TABLE 6.11
Vowel Means Used for Plotting the Vowel Space of Unshifted Speaker
(Peterson and Barney 1952)

Vowel	F_1 Mean (Hz)	F_2 Mean (Hz)
i	310	2790
ɪ	430	2480
eɪ[a]	560	2320
ɛ	610	2330
oʊ[a]	600	1200
u	370	950
ʌ	860	2050
æ	760	1400

a. Because Peterson and Barney (1952) did not provide values for diphthongs, the values for /eɪ/ and /oʊ/ were taken from Stevens (1998).

dialectal backgrounds and of the non-random trends in speakers' utterances" (Peterson and Barney 1952, 175), thus making it a good candidate for a baseline for seeking out dialectal variants.

Front vowels are declared shifted if the mean of the mid values of /i/ or /eɪ/ is closer to the control vowel than it is in the unshifted system or if the mean of mid values of /ɪ/ or /ɛ/ is further from the control vowel than it is in the unshifted system. Ultimately, it was unclear whether /æ/ was also moving as part of the shift, while /ʌ/ appeared relatively stable. Thus, /ʌ/ was used as the control vowel for the Front and Back Shifts. I examined the vowel space

of each of the five women graphically, to show where the vowels are in relation to other vowels in the system.

The graphical representation of Emily's front vowels can be found in
figure 6.9. This figure reveals that /ɛ/ does not appear to be participating in
the SVS for this speaker. That is, it maintains its position with respect to its
tense vowel counterpart and, if anything, seems to appear closer to /ʌ/ than
in the unshifted system. Perhaps this vowel is undergoing a process in opposition to the shift, though such a statement would require numerical veri-
fication. This figure also shows that both /i/ and /eɪ/ are further back and
closer to /ʌ/ than they are in the unshifted system. The graphical representation also shows that /i/ and /ɪ/ have appeared to switch places in terms of
height, suggesting that the shift has at least partially begun in these vowels.

The graphical representation of Hadley's front vowels in figure 6.10
is very similar to Emily's. Both /i/ and /eɪ/ are further back and closer to
/ʌ/ than they are in the unshifted system. Also, /i/ and /ɪ/ appear to have
switched places in terms of height, though not as drastically as Emily's.
Movement of Hadley's /ɛ/ in the F_2 dimension, like that of Emily's, indicates
that this vowel is actually moving back in the mouth, even though the SVS
predicts /ɛ/ will move further forward. For Hadley, /ɛ/ is actually further
back in the mouth than the control vowel, making it more like a mid vowel
than a front one. This is likely due to the fact that Hadley has a rather
fronted /ʌ/ vowel, which suggests that more analysis of these control vowels
is necessary.

For Julie, the results for /ɛ/, /eɪ/, and /ɪ/ resemble those for Emily and
Hadley. The graphical representation in figure 6.11 shows that /i/ and /ɪ/

FIGURE 6.9
Emily's Front Vowels

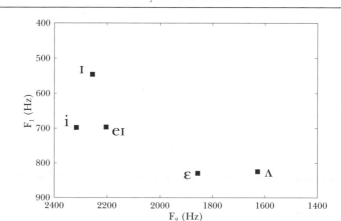

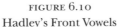

FIGURE 6.10
Hadley's Front Vowels

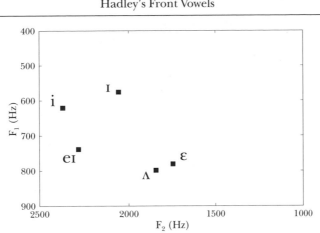

FIGURE 6.11
Julie's Front Vowels

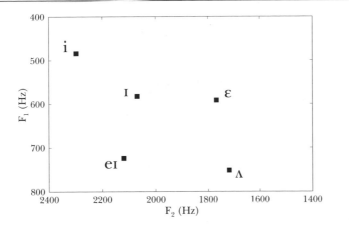

maintain their positions relative to each other. This might be because the lax vowels in Julie's system actually appear to be moving in the opposite direction of the SVS, such that while /i/ is becoming lower and further back in the mouth, /ɪ/ is following the same path. As with the two other women, /ɪ/ is also further back, much closer to the position of the mid vowels, and in this case, /eɪ/ and /ɛ/ have switched positions in terms of height.

The graphical representation of Kellie's front vowels, presented in figure 6.12, shows that, unlike the other three women, the positions of /i/ with respect to /ɪ/ and /eɪ/ with respect to /ɛ/ maintain the expected height/frontness dimensions. Yet, as with the other women, because it appears

FIGURE 6.12
Kellie's Front Vowels

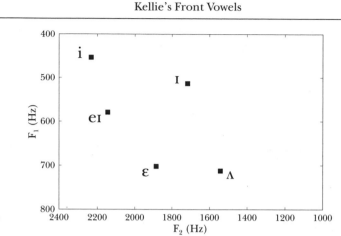

that /ɪ/ and /ɛ/ are actually moving in the opposite direction of the SVS, it is unclear from the graphical representation whether Kellie's vowels are undergoing the processes of the SVS.

In figure 6.13, the graphical representation of Shea's front vowels shows what is expected in the movement of /i/ in a vowel system that is in the process of undergoing the SVS, in that it is much closer to /ɪ/, even though their relative position with respect to height and frontness is maintained, as is the relative position of /eɪ/ and /ɛ/. Again, it appears that at least /ɛ/ and possibly /ɪ/ are moving in the direction opposite to the expectations

FIGURE 6.13
Shea's Front Vowels

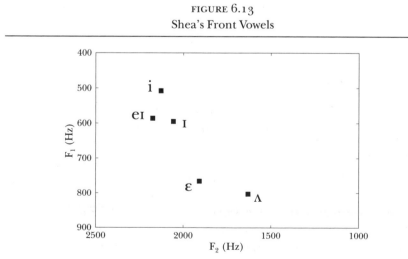

of the SVS. In fact, /ɛ/ is quite close to /ʌ/ and might be better classified as a mid vowel in Shea's system. But at least /i/ appears to be undergoing both expected shifts (in terms of height and backness) in the movement within her system.

What has been discovered in this section is that there appears to be a sort of cline of participation in the Front Shift among these five women. That is, while Emily's and Hadley's vowel systems revealed that /i/ and /eɪ/ are moving back, Julie's and Shea's systems revealed that /eɪ/ is backing but /i/ appears to be both backing and lowering. Kellie, whose speech seems to be most advanced in the SVS, has a system where both /i/ and /eɪ/ appear to be moving in both dimensions. Thus, while Kellie's tense vowels are both falling and backing, the other women's vowels either only move further back or only one vowel moves along both dimensions. One similarity across all speakers is that there does not appear to be any real movement of the two lax front vowels /ɪ/ and /ɛ/ in terms of the SVS.

These results are best understood in light of previous research on the SVS. As Fridland (2000, 268) notes,

Labov's description of the Southern Shift includes two major tendencies: (1) the flip-flop in the position of the tense and lax vowels in the front system, led by the falling of /ey/ [/eɪ/] and subsequent falling of /iy/ [/i/], and the monophthongization of /ay/ [/aɪ/]; and (2) the fronting of several of the back vowels.

This means that, in the Front Shift, /eɪ/ falls first, then /i/ falls. The results of the current study seem to indicate that, if taking the most conservative systems as the starting points of the shift, the backing of these two vowels happens first. Additionally, while the most active changes in Fridland's study were occurring in /eɪ/ and /ɛ/ (other shifts were noted as rare in that study), this study seems to indicate that the backing of /eɪ/ and /i/ leads the shift, followed by the lowering of /i/ and then the lowering of /eɪ/, as in the most radical system of Kellie.

How can these differences from previous studies be explained? One explanation might be found in the particular population from which these data were drawn. One might describe these subjects as young, (upper-) middle- to upper-class women, resembling some of the upper-class speakers in Feagin's (1986) study in Alabama. Fridland (1998, 62) points out that Feagin's results with upper class speakers suggest "that the changes occurring in Southern speech are perhaps being adopted as incoming norms from below and have not yet reached the level of conscious awareness which might cause them to be suppressed." Thus, the changes might be occurring in a different pattern than found in other socioeconomic groups in previous studies.

Despite the fact that the order in which the shift is taking place is different for these women, it is important to note that the shift is at least partially taking place. This indicates that (1) the shift has at least partially made its way into urban centers, as Fridland (2000, 2001) also showed with Memphis, (2) these Louisvillians have access to features that have been fairly well contained within Southern dialects, and (3) there are varying levels of participation in the shift, even among a rather homogenous group (young, female, higher socioeconomic class), which is also indicative of the border nature of the city.

6.1.3. FRONTING OF BACK VOWELS. In this section, I again follow the methodology of Fridland (cf. 1998; 2000; 2001) in examining the movement of the back vowels in the SVS. Using the same unshifted speaker as presented in figure 6.8, this section examines the speech of each woman in order to determine the level of participation in the Back Shift.

Back vowels are declared shifted if the mean of the mid values of /u/ or /oʊ/ is closer to the control vowel /ʌ/ than it is in the unshifted system. Even though the shift has been mostly described in terms of fronting, this section also examines the level to which these vowels may also be lowering. As with the Front Shift, I present graphical representations of the vowel space for each woman to gauge participation in the shift.

The graphical representation of Emily's back vowels can be seen in figure 6.14. Here it is clear that while /oʊ/ maintains its position behind /ʌ/, though closer than in the unshifted system, /u/ has fronted to the point that it is in front of /ʌ/, perhaps more appropriately being characterized

FIGURE 6.14
Emily's Back Vowels

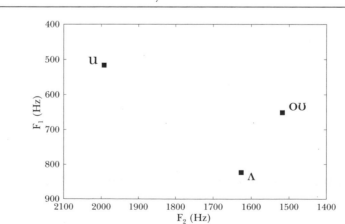

as a front vowel. There appears to be no change in terms of the height of these vowels.

Figure 6.15 is the graphical representation of Hadley's back vowels. As with Emily, it appears that Hadley's /u/ has moved so far to the front so as to be in front of the control vowel /ʌ/. This indicates significant fronting of this vowel, as I noted in the Front Shift that it is likely that Hadley's /ʌ/ vowel has fronted as well. Also, /oʊ/ has fallen so far so as to be below /ʌ/, which is not true in the unshifted speaker. The image also reveals that /oʊ/ might also be closer to /ʌ/ than in the unshifted system, which might indicate that it is moving forward as well.

As with Emily and Hadley, Julie's vowel space in figure 6.16 shows that /u/ has fronted to the point that it might be better described as a front vowel, as it is quite far in front of the mid control vowel. However, the position of /oʊ/ with respect to /ʌ/ seems to be more like the expected distance in the unshifted system. Julie's vowel system looks quite a lot like Emily's in terms of the height and frontness dimensions of these vowels with respect to the control vowel.

The graphical representation of Kellie's vowel system can be found in figure 6.17. In this figure, /u/ is clearly in a front position, as was the case with the other women, such that it has not only moved forward toward /ʌ/, but has actually passed it. On the other hand, /oʊ/ also appears to be moving forward, unlike in the systems of the other women, though it has not passed the control vowel to the same extent as /u/. It also appears that these vowels have lowered with respect to the control vowel, as the height

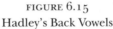

FIGURE 6.15
Hadley's Back Vowels

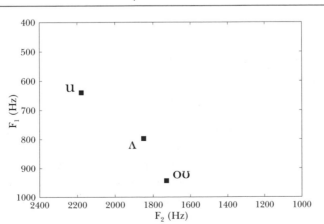

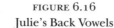

FIGURE 6.16
Julie's Back Vowels

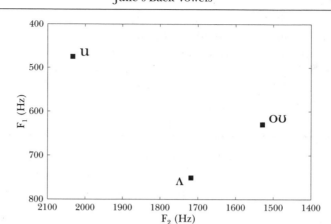

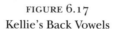

FIGURE 6.17
Kellie's Back Vowels

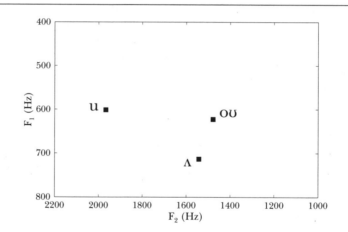

distance between these vowels and the control vowel appears to be much smaller than the distance in the unshifted system.

Finally, I examine the back vowels in Shea's system, presented in figure 6.18. Here, it is clear that, as with all of the other women, /u/ has moved so far to the front to have passed /ʌ/ and become what might be better described as a front vowel. Yet, unlike the other women, Shea's /oʊ/ vowel has moved so far forward so as to no longer hold a position strictly behind the control vowel but basically directly above it, so as to be more like a central vowel. The image also shows that it is likely that these vowels are lowering with respect to the control vowel.

FIGURE 6.18
Shea's Back Vowels

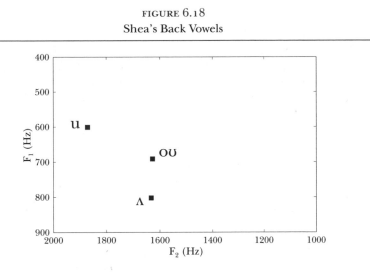

As with the Front Shift, there is some variation among these women in their participation in the Back Shift. For all of the women, /u/ is fronted significantly, so as to be in front of the control vowel, inhabiting the space typically reserved for front vowels. However, while Kellie's and Shea's systems reveal the most extreme case, where both /u/ and /ou/ are both fronting and falling, Emily's and Julie's systems showed movement forward for /u/ and /ou/, but no lowering for these two vowels. Hadley's system appears to be a bit anomalous in terms of the Back Shift, in that while /u/ is fronting as in the other systems, /ou/ is only lowering and not moving forward as anticipated by this shift.

The movement of /u/ has been noted as the first shift of the Back Shift. As Fridland (2000) noted, the advancement of /ou/, while parallel to that of /u/, is much smaller than that of /u/. In the Memphis study, Fridland found that the most advanced systems feature /u/ as being in front of /ʌ/, sometimes overlapping with front vowels. This is also true of the data I present here.

Hadley's seemingly anomalous system is also represented in the results of Fridland's Memphis study: "There is also evidence that the /ow/ [/ou/] class is both falling and fronting, with fronting less advanced that [*sic*] falling in that class according to the means but not significantly in paired t-test results" (Fridland 1998, 437). Since fronting is less advanced for the /ou/ class, the fact that this vowel only appears to be lowering is not so surprising.

What is found with the Back Shift is similar to what was found with the Front Shift and with /aɪ/-monophthongization. That is, the women vary in their use and nonuse of the Southern variants, yet they appear to have the variables in their inventory. Considering all of these aspects of the SVS, these results indicate that the speakers analyzed here can be best described as being on a cline of participation in terms of the vowel movements. From these results, it appears that Kellie has the most advanced Southern system, positioning her at the high end of the cline, while Hadley, who has the least amount of Southern features, would be positioned near the low end of the cline. Between these two women, Shea, Julie, and Emily would be represented as having the most to least advanced systems, respectively.

6.1.4. PIN/PEN MERGER. In addition to the SVS, a common dialect feature for Southern speakers is the merger of the front-lax vowels /ɛ/ and /ɪ/ before nasal consonants. The method of analysis for this and the following section draws heavily on Hazen's (2005) research in West Virginia, another border location where both the PIN/PEN and the COT/CAUGHT mergers were found. As such, for the PIN/PEN merger, vowel tokens were extracted from single syllable words wherein the vowel under investigation appeared in noninitial position before [n] or [m]. Vowels were subjected to spectral analysis, and for each speaker, both a qualitative and a quantitative view of the merger is presented. For the qualitative view, I present plots of the vowel space based on extracted F_1 and F_2 values from midpoints of individual tokens for each speaker such that the presence of overlapping tokens suggests that the merger has taken place. For the quantitative view, statistical analyses (independent sample t-tests and confidence intervals) of the F_1 and F_2 values for each pair of vowels for each speaker are presented. For this merger, individual speakers are again compared to Peterson and Barney's unshifted female, who exhibited a mean difference between /ɪ/ and /ɛ/ of 180Hz in F_1 and 150Hz in F_2.

Ten tokens of each vowel in Emily's speech can be seen in figure 6.19. This image reveals that many of the tokens of prenasal /ɪ/ and /ɛ/ overlap for this speaker. Indeed, there are at least four pairs of tokens that exhibit individual near-complete overlap. An examination of the median values for F_1 and F_2 for these vowels for Emily reveals that these vowels differ by only 10 Hz in the F_1 dimension and 100 Hz in the F_2 dimension. This speaker appears to have a near complete merger, at least in terms of vowel height.

Tokens taken from Hadley's speech are represented in figure 6.20. Like Emily's tokens, Hadley's prenasal /ɪ/ and /ɛ/ vowels seem to have extensive overlap. The median values of F_1 for the two vowels differ by 12 Hz, while the median values differ by 59 Hz in F_2. Hadley's vowels are similar to Emily's in terms of height, but Hadley's vowels are closer together than Emily's in terms of vowel frontness.

FIGURE 6.19
Emily's Prenasal /ɪ/ and /ɛ/ Tokens

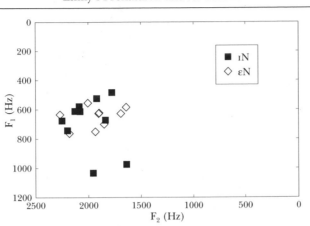

FIGURE 6.20
Hadley's Prenasal /ɪ/ and /ɛ/ Tokens

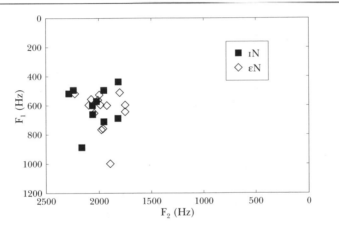

Julie's prenasal /ɪ/ and /ɛ/ tokens, displayed in figure 6.21, also show a fairly high level of overlap for the two vowels. The level of difference in the median values of the vowels in F_1 is slightly higher than Emily's and Hadley's, at 60 Hz, but the F_2 values are closer for Julie, at a difference of only 42 Hz, thus making this dimension similar between Julie and Hadley.

Kellie's prenasal vowels, pictured in figure 6.22, seem much more dispersed in the vowel space than the other three women's, but an examination of the median values again reveals a high level of participation in the merger. The difference between the two vowels in the F_1 dimension is 35 Hz, and the difference between the two vowels in the F_2 dimension is 39 Hz.

FIGURE 6.21
Julie's Prenasal /ɪ/ and /ɛ/ Tokens

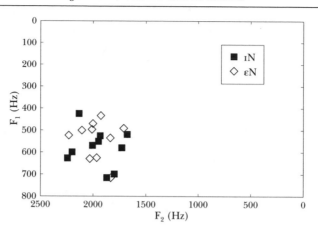

FIGURE 6.22
Kellie's Prenasal /ɪ/ and /ɛ/ Tokens

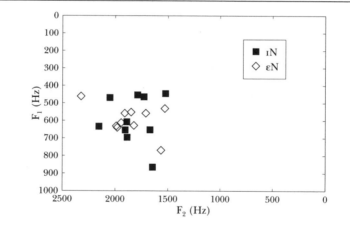

These two vowels appear to be very similar in both the height and frontness dimensions.

The prenasal vowel tokens produced by Shea are featured in figure 6.23. Of the vowel systems presented in this section, it can be argued that Shea's, while still exhibiting a good deal of overlap, also features clearly separate patterns for these two vowels, such that the /ɪ/ tokens cluster together for the most part in the space above the /ɛ/ tokens. Indeed, Shea's vowels feature the highest level of difference of these five women in F_1 dimension at 88 Hz, though the difference in F_2 is 36 Hz, which is comparable to other values presented here.

FIGURE 6.23
Shea's Prenasal /ɪ/ and /ɛ/ Tokens

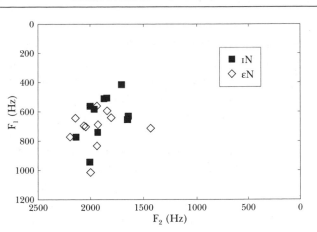

These qualitative patterns are also apparent in the statistical analyses. Independent sample *t*-tests comparing each individual here with the Peterson and Barney unshifted female were conducted, the results of which are presented in table 6.12. A significant result indicates that the speaker exhibits the merger in the dimension under consideration (F_1 or F_2, considered separately). These results show that two of these women (Julie and Kellie) are fully merged in both dimensions, while the other three women are merged in at least one dimension (F_1 for Emily and Hadley, F_2 for Shea).

The results do not align with previous work in Louisville that has suggested the feature is not found there (Labov, Ash, and Boberg 2006). Indeed, for two speakers, the merger is complete, while it appears to be in progress for the other three. Perhaps this is a change in progress, one that suggests a more rural feature making its way into urban centers via

TABLE 6.12
Statistical Analysis for PIN-PEN Merger

	F_1			F_2		
		95% CI			*95% CI*	
	p-value	*(low)*	*(high)*	*p-value*	*(low)*	*(high)*
Emily	.010*	−126	121	.145	−94	205
Hadley	.007*	−64	126	.123	−31	183
Julie	< .001*	−105	29	.028*	−144	126
Kellie	.001*	−87	90	.033*	−201	129
Shea	.067	−24	190	.009*	−201	80

*$p < .05$

contrahierarchical diffusion (G. Bailey et al. 1993). Regardless, the results indicate that this linguistic resource is available, at least to some degree, for Louisvillians.

6.1.5. COT/CAUGHT MERGER. Finally, in addition to exploring the data for evidence of Southern dialect features, I turn to the low back vowel merger, a feature that has typically been resisted in Southern dialects but is found in some Midwestern communities near Louisville. As with the PIN/PEN merger, I have produced an analysis that draws on the methods described in Hazen (2005). In this case, vowel tokens were extracted from single syllable words wherein the vowel appeared in noninitial position before [t] or [k]. Vowels were subjected to spectral analysis, and again for each speaker, both a qualitative and a quantitative view of the merger are presented. For this merger, individual speakers are again compared to Peterson and Barney's unshifted female, who exhibited a mean difference between /ɑ/ and /ɔ/ of 260 Hz in F_1 and 300 Hz in F_2.

Emily's low back vowel tokens can be seen in figure 6.24. Impressionistically, Emily's tokens seem to exhibit a fairly clear separation between the two vowels, such that most of the /ɔ/ tokens appear higher and backer than the /ɑ/ tokens. There are several instances of overlap, however. The difference in F_1 for the median values of these values is 161 Hz, and the difference in F_2 is 96 Hz.

Figure 6.25 features low back vowel tokens taken from Hadley's speech. This image looks quite similar to many of the ones presented for the PIN/PEN merger, and there is a considerable amount of overlap. The median

FIGURE 6.24
Emily's /ɑ/ and /ɔ/ Tokens

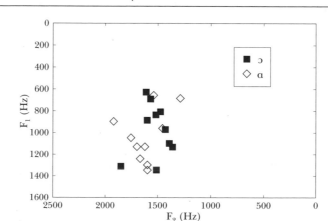

FIGURE 6.25
Hadley's /ɑ/ and /ɔ/ Tokens

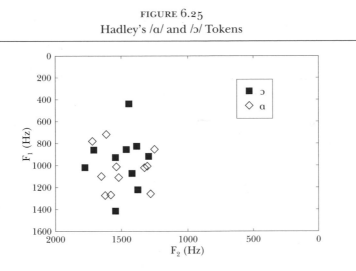

values for Hadley's vowels differ such that this difference is smaller than with Emily's vowels (100 Hz in F_1, 82 Hz in F_2). The impression of merger aligns with this fact.

Similarly, Julie's low back vowel tokens exhibit overlap, as seen in figure 6.26. The image of merger presented here is mirrored in the fact that the vowels only differ in height by 64 Hz and in frontness by 15 Hz.

Kellie's low back vowels, like Emily's, look as though the vowels have somewhat distinct patterns despite some amount of overlap, as seen in figure 6.27. Kellie's /ɔ/ tokens are further back than her /ɑ/ tokens, though

FIGURE 6.26
Julie's /ɑ/ and /ɔ/ Tokens

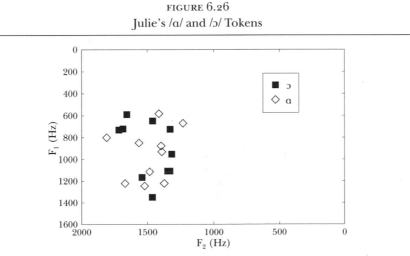

FIGURE 6.27
Kellie's /ɑ/ and /ɔ/ Tokens

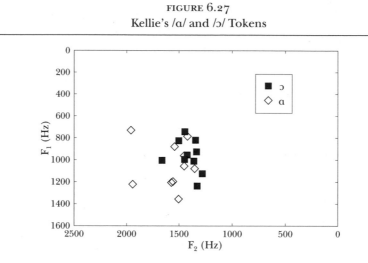

they do not appear to differ very much in height. The difference in the median values of these vowels in the F_1 dimension is 93 Hz and is 132 Hz in the F_2 dimension. Thus, the two vowels in Kellie's system are both qualitatively and quantitatively closer together in terms of height.

The vowel tokens from Shea's speech are presented in figure 6.28. As with some of the other images, the overlap between the vowels is visually eclipsed by the tendency for the /ɔ/ vowels to cluster separately from the /ɑ/ vowels. The difference in median values between /ɔ/ and /ɑ/ is 26 Hz in F_1 and 107 Hz in F_2 for Shea.

FIGURE 6.28
Shea's /ɑ/ and /ɔ/ Tokens

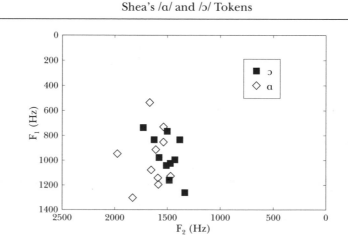

TABLE 6.13
Statistical Analysis for COT-CAUGHT Merger

| | F_1 | | | | F_2 | | |
| | | 95% CI | | | | 95% CI | |
	p-value	(low)	(high)	p-value		(low)	(high)
Emily	.050*	−118	260	.003*		−42	203
Hadley	.049*	−92	258	< .001*		−124	114
Julie	.035*	−150	238	< .001*		−123	122
Kellie	.021*	−54	224	.042*		30	293
Shea	.010*	−138	181	.008*		34	245

*$p < .05$.

Interestingly, these qualitative patterns, wherein vowels tended to exhibit visual separation, are not found in the statistical analyses. The results of independent sample *t*-tests comparing each individual with the Peterson and Barney unshifted female are presented in table 6.13. As with the PIN/PEN merger, a significant result indicates that the speaker exhibits the merger in the dimension under consideration (F_1 or F_2, considered separately). These results show that all women are fully merged for these vowels.

These results also do not align with previous work in Louisville, which has suggested these vowels remain unmerged (Labov, Ash, and Boberg 2006). At least in the phonetic contexts examined here, this merger appears to be complete. Since these two mergers have been thought to be mutually exclusive in most American contexts, the fact that these five women exhibit both mergers to varying degrees is quite interesting. Perhaps this population is comparable to the West Virginian population studied by Hazen (2005, 216), who suggested that, at least in these border locales, there may be "a future period where having both mergers is the norm." Thus, the presence of both mergers simultaneously marks Louisvillians at least partially as both Southern and non-Southern.

6.2. EXPRESSIONS OF SOUTHERNNESS IN CONTEXT

How can the variable use of these variants be explained? I argue that Louisville's location in the proximity of Southern dialects gives the women access to these features, yet their use is at least partially context driven. In this section, I present several instances of the use of the monophthongal variant of /aɪ/, which has been shown to coincide with an expression of Southern identity (Feagin 2000), in context. The analysis of the discourse in this way can reveal how, in a particular moment, a speaker creates for herself an expression of her regional identity. It is expected that context can determine the choice of a particular variant, particularly in a context where one's regional identity becomes important and small phonetic details can serve as implicit signs of belonging within that group. The focus will be on monophthongization of /aɪ/ because of its strong association with Southernness.[8]

It is quite common for Southerners to use the monophthongal variant in words related to the first-person singular pronoun (e.g., *I*, *I'll*, *I'm*, *my*, etc.) as an expression of Southern identity (Feagin 2000). The speakers in this study varied in their use of the monophthong in these words, as summarized in table 6.14.

In most of these situations, the topic of interest was not so much about being Southern, but more about regular, mundane activities: Shea's use of *I'm* appeared in the context of a discussion about make-up; Julie uses *I* to report her location at a particular restaurant; and Kellie uses *I* to provide a pleasant response to Emily's new haircut. A clear example of the mundane

TABLE 6.14
Summary of Monophthong Use in First-Person Singular Words

	Words	*Monophthong in F_1?*	*Monophthong in F_2?*
Emily	I	FALSE	TRUE
	I'm	TRUE	TRUE
	my	TRUE	TRUE
	I've	FALSE	FALSE
Hadley	I	TRUE	TRUE
	I've	TRUE	TRUE
	my	TRUE	FALSE
	I'm	FALSE	TRUE
	I'll	FALSE	FALSE
Julie	I	FALSE	FALSE
	I'm	TRUE	TRUE
	I'll	TRUE	TRUE
	my	TRUE	TRUE
Kellie	I	TRUE	TRUE
	my	FALSE	TRUE
	I'm	FALSE	TRUE
Shea	I've	TRUE	TRUE
	I	FALSE	TRUE
	I'm	FALSE	TRUE
	my	FALSE	FALSE

activities discussed while using the monophthongal variant can be seen in one instance of Hadley's use of *I*, highlighted in (1).[9]

> 1. I really just want to show off my dog and have people tell me how cute he is. Because I know he is. So, we walk past Dot Fox, favorite store, and I was like, "Let's just hop in, you know, I heard they're having a sale." [Hadley (to camera)]

But an example of where the topic seems to be of great import to the individual identity of the speaker can be seen in Emily's use of the word *I'm*, which was determined to be a monophthong in both F_1 and F_2. It is used in a context where Emily is describing her dreams for success as a journalist, in (2).

> 2. All through college, I was getting up at four in the morning. I definitely made some sacrifices along the way. You have to in order to have any kind of success. I'm livin' my own dream, I'm not livin' anyone else's. I'm doin' what I wanna do. [Emily (to camera)]

This example is interesting in that, in the production of a sentence dealing clearly with identity issues, the first-person singular pronoun surfaces as the Southern variant. Given that Emily has the ability to produce nonmonophthongal versions of /aɪ/, the use of the Southern variant in this context emerges as a linguistic act of identity (Le Page and Tabouret-Keller 1985), indicating an inherent connection between her identity at this moment and Southernness.

Contexts where the speaker's "real" or vernacular speech is likely to arise include instances where the speaker is paying little attention to their speech, as in discussions of their fear of dying or other emotional situations (e.g., Labov 1972). For Shea, this occurs when she reveals that she has recently suffered two rather sad events, in (3).

> 3. Jeff and I were going through a rough patch, and he was sort of disappearing on me. I knew I was being lied to. The two biggest surprises of my entire life both happened in the same week. My fiancé cheated on me and my mom died. I lost my mother and my best friend. [Shea (to camera)]

In this instance, Shea, who is visibly distraught, reveals her sad news, and in doing so, she uses the standard /aɪ/ diphthong, not the monophthong, in her production of *my*. While the fact that she is speaking on camera, a situation that likely requires some attention to speech, might have created the actual context for her usage, it is important to note also that Shea rarely shows this level of emotion throughout the course of the show.

At one point, she even comments that she does not cry. Yet, in this instance, Shea is clearly upset, and her use of the diphthongal variant might be best linked to her understanding of the seriousness of the issue, not necessarily with her expression of Southernness.

Examples (4) and (5) from Kellie's speech represent two utterances over the course of a short period of time, where Kellie is trying to set her mom up on a date with a man she meets at a coffee shop. In both of these utterances, Kellie uses the monophthongal variant.

4. Oh, good! I'm very excited. I'm Kellie. [Kellie (to man)]
5. Um! [laughter] If you are up for it, would you like to go on a date with my momma? [Kellie (to man)]

What is different about this case is that Kellie is not talking to the camera. She is talking to another person with whom she would like to build a connection. In both making an introduction of herself in (4), an expression clearly linked to one's personal identity, and her mention of her mother in (5), another likely context connected closely to Kellie's identity, Kellie produces at least a partially monophthongal vowel (both of which were perceived to be monophthongal in my auditory analysis). This use indicates that Kellie may be attempting to present herself as a Southerner to this man, something she must assume he will appreciate, since she is trying to get him to do something for her. This expression of Southernness, then, appears in the context of Kellie's attempt to be real, friendly, and hospitable in order to get what she wants.

Moving beyond the words that are related to *I*, Julie's use of the monophthongal variant in her production of *sometimes* can be seen in (6). This word, uttered in front of the camera, comes in the context of Julie being set up by Kellie on a second blind date after having already been rejected.

6. Sometimes you have to be vulnerable in order to make yourself available for good things to happen. [Julie (to camera)]

Julie's vulnerability is made explicit through this statement, yet she hopes to acknowledge that one has to try in order to succeed. This vulnerability might also be described in terms of being emotional, a situation where the vernacular is likely to arise. Julie's use of the monophthongal variant in this context reveals that her vulnerability is expressed through the use of Southern vowels.

This section has shown that, particularly with the first-person pronoun examples, the use of the monophthongal variant is rather varied. Contexts where identity is key or where emotions run deep seem to trigger the use of the Southern vowels, though perhaps seriousness or other situations require the use of the standard variant (see Mishoe 1995; Cramer 2015b).

It is not completely clear that these women draw distinctions between contexts for expressing Southernness and contexts for not. The seemingly random use or nonuse of the Southern variant further indicates the fluidity and dynamicity of the border situation, such that the choice in variant is both chaotic and complex for these speakers. The situation appears similar to that found in Negrón's (2014, 114) work with two speakers negotiating what it means to be Latino, wherein "it is more apt to see their negotiation of shared latinidad as drawing from a set of distinctive features from a range of ethnolinguistic repertoires." One might say, then, that the women whose speech was analyzed in this chapter are merely negotiating what it means to be Louisvillian through their selection of differing linguistic variants.

6.3. DISCUSSION

This chapter has shown that the use or nonuse of the Southern and non-Southern vowel variants is not straightforward. I would argue that the most appropriate explanation for the variation in the results of the qualitative, quantitative, and contextual analyses is that Louisville's position on the border between two distinct dialects, one that includes Southern features and one that does not, makes it such that these women have access to both sets of features, and the fluidity with which they approach their regional identity is represented in their seemingly random selection of vowel variants.

An important feature that hints to this argument is the homogenous nature of the group investigated here. These speakers are all young females who form a coherent friendship group and who live upwardly mobile lives in the high society circles of Louisville. One might expect, in a group of such similar types, to find rather similar and consistent results. However, these results show that these linguistic identities are not so secure, as indicated by their varying performances of regionality. Within the context of the border, however, this is not unexpected; the rather dynamic way in which these women produce the signs of regional identity discussed here is anticipated by the fact that they are located in a place between places.

Overall, this chapter has examined how regional identity is realized linguistically through the use or nonuse of Southern and non-Southern vowel variants. It indicates that the use of Southern features is in line with Labov, Ash, and Boberg's (2006) description of Louisville, where only 50% of respondents used the monophthongal variant of /aɪ/, the feature they use to define the Southern dialect region. Thus, like with the perception of regionality in Louisville, it appears that the linguistic production of regional identity is also complex and unclear.

7. THE FLUIDITY
OF REGIONAL IDENTITY

FACTS OF GEOGRAPHY easily place Louisville in the middle of everything. For example, in a Brookings Institute case study involving Louisville, the city is described as follows:

Centrally located on the southern banks of the Ohio River, amid an agriculturally productive, mineral rich, and energy producing region, Louisville is commonly described as the northernmost city of the American South. Closer to Toronto than to New Orleans, and even slightly closer to Chicago than to Atlanta, it remains within a day's drive of two-thirds of the American population living east of the Rocky Mountains. [Bennett and Gatz 2008, 3]

And it is this geography in combination with the many other kinds of middle-of-the-road depictions of Louisville discussed in this book that make the city a prime location for the investigation of the fluidity of regional identity. In this book, I have shown the split, mixed nature of the regional linguistic identities in and of Louisville. The data presented in this book exhibit a convergence of identities in the city, with Louisvillians appearing conflicted as to their own place and with non-Louisvillians casting their urban neighbors as clearly the other in the state. Louisvillians are seen as Southern and non-Southern in many different ways; for example, in describing how Louisvillians see national, regional, and statewide variation broadly, Southernness (and, more specifically, Appalachianness) is often denigrated by Louisvillians, even though, when exploring where Louisvillians position themselves in this landscape, they associate the more positive stereotypes about with those regions (e.g., pleasantness, hospitality) with their own variety. In their view, Louisville speech can be seen as exhibiting the best of what the nearby regions have to offer. It is educated and correct, like nearby Midwestern varieties, but participants also distance themselves from the features of Midwestern speech that they do not value (e.g., rudeness, fast paced lives).

The major way in which they classify Louisville in terms of statewide variation is as separate from the rest of the state. This is also the most common way in which non-Louisvillian Kentuckians describe the state's largest urban center in terms of regional linguistic identity. While still connecting educated, standard speech to the Louisville area, something they do not ascribe to the non-urban portions of the state, non-Louisvillians describe the city as being not Kentucky enough.

In terms of the production of regional identity through linguistic means, the use or nonuse of Southern linguistic features was shown to be anything but straightforward. The results suggest that context need not be the deciding factor for use of a Southern vowel, in that speakers use the Southern vowels in numerous contexts, but they also shift to the standard diphthongal form for unclear identity functions. It is argued that Louisville's position on the border between two dialects, one that uses the Southern vowels and one that does not, creates a scenario where speakers have access to both sets of vowels, and their fluid regional identities are represented in the seemingly random selection of vowel variants.

My goals in this study were clear. I intended to show that the regional identity produced and perceived by and about Louisvillians is not simple nor straightforward because of its location at a border. The impact of the border is seen in the linguistic acts of identities explored herein. The conflict and contradiction found in anthropological studies of borderlands (i.e., Alvarez 1995) was found in this community as well with respect to its linguistic identities. We have seen a lack of uniformity in how Louisvillians express themselves and in how non-Louisvillians categorize people from this city. We have examined the Southern and non-Southern tendencies of Louisvillians, indicating a convergence and multiplicity of identities. Louisvillians seem to relish their middle-ground status.

These results have several implications for (socio)linguistic research. Overall, this research project provides a broader understanding of the linguistic situation in Louisville, which indicates that large-scale dialectological surveys are in need of more local studies, like this one, to better understand internal variation. Thus, communities on isoglosses would prove to be extremely important and interesting locales for these types of indepth studies because, based on this project, borderlands appear to be important locations for the examination of identity, specifically as it relates to language perception and use.

Beyond these implications, this book also showcases the particular empirical, theoretical, and methodological advances this research makes to the field of sociolinguistics. In terms of empirical contributions, as indicated in chapter 2, little research has focused expansively on Louisville. As such, one of my goals in conducting this research was to put Louisville on the map, as it were, of linguistic research. In addition to being understudied more broadly, Louisville has not been fully considered in folk linguistic research either. This project expands upon the current framework and lays the groundwork to be taken up in further similar studies. The attention paid to borders in this research can be considered an empirical advancement as well in that, despite the salience of these borders for many Americans, little research has considered their impact on regional linguistic identities, and this work sheds some light on problems associated with the notion of static regionality.

Despite the fact that many linguists have not considered the views of nonlinguists to be "real" linguistic data, this project shows that the analysis of phonetic data is complemented well by the analysis of mental map and perceptual data. For instance, the analysis of the production data revealed mixed results in terms of whether the vowels produced were Southern or non-Southern. These results were mirrored in the analysis of the mental maps and the perceptual data, which shows that the perceptions align well with the production data. Yet, the perceptual data revealed further that the stereotypes associated with Southern speech often conditioned the participants' responses more toward considering themselves to be Midwestern. Without the views of the nonlinguists, this research project would only describe half of the picture.

I would argue, however, that the largest contributions of this work are methodological. The methodology used in this research project was multidimensional, drawing insights from sociolinguistics, linguistic anthropology, and folk linguistics in order to provide a better overall framework for examining the situation in Louisville, and it provides a systematic way of addressing both the production and perception of regional identity, combining a quantitative and a qualitative approach to data analysis. This project furthers our understanding of regionality and linguistic identities at regional, dialect, and other types of borders. Additionally, the inclusion of work from anthropology, particularly the research that deals with the dynamicity of culture at the border, enhances the approach to the data. In fact, the theoretical framework used here would be rather appropriate in the consideration of other border situations, thus providing the theoretical understanding necessary for the complexity and fluidity of identities at the border.

A broader advance discussed in this volume is the use of Geographic Information System (GIS) technologies in perceptual dialectology research. While Preston has noted that digitization of hand-drawn maps is possible by tracing these maps onto digitizing pads (e.g., Preston and Howe 1987), the approach used in this volume is a more mobile and cost-effective method that makes the data more easily quantified and creates images that are more appealing. At the beginning of this research project, such methods were not used; the shift toward GIS-centered perceptual dialectology is taking place now (e.g., Montgomery and Stoeckle 2013, Cramer and Montgomery 2016), and I would suggest that it is important for researchers in this field (and others) to work together to shape this new methodology and push forward with best practices for utilizing such tools in the analysis of (socio)linguistic data.

Yet, there is more work to be done. In addition to Louisville, it is important that other border communities be examined utilizing the methods exploited in this research project. It would be particularly interesting to examine other communities along the Ohio River, since it seems to be the natural dividing line between Southern and non-Southern regions. It might also be helpful to understand more clearly the views directly across the river, so that the ways in which regional identity is produced and perceived on either side of the line can be compared. For example, though Preston (e.g., 1989) has already examined the community in southern Indiana, the next step might be to further compare their perceptions to those in Louisville. Further research like this, as well as with other Kentucky border situations, like Cincinnati and northern Kentucky, or Evansville, Indiana, and Henderson, Kentucky, would show exactly how real of a border the Ohio River is for people in these communities.

Additionally, research with communities further away from Louisville, outside of Kentucky, might also show how salient the Ohio River is as a border in the dialect landscape of the United States. People in Louisville often lament, as some did on the survey, that if they go north of Louisville, people are certain they are from the South, but if they go south of Louisville, people might consider them a Midwesterner. These travel experiences could be borne out in studies that attempt to elucidate where people outside of Louisville, or its immediate area, place the city in terms of region.

Ultimately, I believe this book has painted a clear picture of an unclear situation. Louisvillians appear to exhibit both Southern and non-Southern identities in their production and perception of regional identity through varying alignments, revealing the contested and dynamic nature of identity in the borderlands. The border serves as a major factor in how Louisvillians produce and perceive regional variation and in how Louisvillians are characterized by others. This project shows that a better understanding of how regional identity is produced and perceived in border regions of the United States can be had, and more research into these kinds of identity alignments will greatly improve how we understand regionality and variation more broadly.

APPENDIX

Label: _____

1. How **different** is this way of speaking from **your own** way of speaking?

1	2	3	4
Same	A little different	Somewhat different	Different

2. How **correct** is this way of speaking?

1	2	3	4
Correct	Mostly correct	Not very correct	Incorrect

3. How **pleasant** is this way of speaking?

1	2	3	4
Pleasant	Mostly pleasant	Not very pleasant	Unpleasant

4. How **standard** is this way of speaking?

1	2	3	4
Standard	Mostly standard	Not very standard	Nonstandard

5. How **formal** is this way of speaking?

1	2	3	4
Formal	Mostly formal	Not very formal	Informal

6. How **beautiful** is this way of speaking?

1	2	3	4
Beautiful	Mostly beautiful	Not very beautiful	Ugly

7. How **educated** is this way of speaking?

1	2	3	4
Educated	Mostly educated	Not very educated	Uneducated

8. How else might you describe this way of speaking?

9. Why did you select this label for this way of speaking?

10. What does this label mean to you?

INFORMATION ABOUT INDIVIDUAL LOUISVILLE
PARTICIPANTS IN REGIONAL STUDY

No.	Age	Sex	Education	Income	Birthplace	Year in Louisville
1	40	F	post-graduate degree	$75,000–100,000	Louisville	40
2	35	F	post-graduate degree	$50,000–75,000	Louisville	35
3	64	M	post-graduate degree	$100,000–125,000	Louisville	35
4	38	M	post-graduate degree	$25,000–50,000	Louisville	35
5	61	M	post-graduate degree	$75,000–100,000	Louisville	35
6	31	M	post-graduate degree	$25,000–50,000	Louisville	35
7	30	M	post-graduate degree	$75,000–100,000	Louisville	35
8	60	F	post-graduate degree	—	Louisville	35
9	23	M	4-year degree	$50,000–75,000	Louisville	35
10	66	M	post-graduate degree	$50,000–75,000	Brooklyn, N.Y.	35
11	28	M	post-graduate degree	less than $25,000	Louisville	35
12	18	M	some college	$50,000–75,000	Louisville	35
13	19	M	some college	—	Flint, Mich.	35
14	23	M	high school/GED	$50,000–75,000	Louisville	35
15	19	M	high school/GED	$100,000–125,000	Louisville	35
16	54	M	high school/GED	$100,000–125,000	Louisville	35
17	44	F	2-year degree	$75,000–100,000	California	35
18	37	F	post-graduate degree	—	Louisville	35
19	50	F	post-graduate degree	$100,000–125,000	Louisville	35
20	48	F	2-year degree	$75,000–100,000	Middlesboro, Ky.	35
21	51	F	4-year degree	—	Indianapolis, Ind.	35
22	51	F	high school/GED	$25,000–50,000	Louisville	35
23	23	F	4-year degree	$25,000–50,000	Louisville	35

SUMMARY INFORMATION ABOUT LOUISVILLE
PARTICIPANTS IN REGIONAL STUDY

Gender

Female	10	43.5%
Male	13	56.5%
TOTAL	23	

Education

Less than high school	0	0.0%
High school/GED	4	17.4%
Some college	2	8.7%
2-year degree	2	8.7%
4-year degree	3	13.0%
Some post-graduate	0	0.0%
Post-graduate degree	12	52.2%
TOTAL	23	

Income

Less than $25,000	1	4.3%
$25,000–50,000	4	17.4%
$50,000–75,000	5	21.7%
$75,000–100,000	5	21.7%
$100,000–125,000	4	17.4%
$125,000–150,000	0	0.0%
More than $150,000	0	0.0%
Omitted	4	17.4%
TOTAL	23	

SUMMARY INFORMATION ABOUT KENTUCKIAN PARTICIPANTS IN STATE-ONLY STUDY

Gender		
Female	135	54.0%
Male	113	44.2%
Omitted	2	0.8%
TOTAL	250	

Education		
Less than high school	5	2.0%
High school/GED	36	14.4%
Some college	130	52.0%
2-year degree	14	5.6%
4-year degree	35	14.0%
Some post-graduate	6	2.4%
Post-graduate degree	22	8.8%
Other	1	0.4%
Omitted	1	0.4%
TOTAL	250	

Income		
Less than $25,000	98	39.2%
$25,000–50,000	39	15.6%
$50,000–75,000	19	7.6%
$75,000–100,000	22	8.8%
$100,000–125,000	12	4.8%
$125,000–150,000	9	3.6%
More than $150,000	12	4.8%
Omitted	39	15.6%
TOTAL	250	

Race/Ethnicity		
White	222	88.8%
African-American	21	8.4%
Hispanic	0	0.0%
Native American	0	0.0%
Other	7	2.8%
TOTAL	250	

SUMMARY INFORMATION ABOUT PARTICIPANTS IN ONLINE SURVEY OF LANGUAGE ATTITUDES

Gender		
Female	47	69.1%
Male	21	30.9%
TOTAL	68	

Education		
High school	3	4.4%
Some college	9	13.2%
Post-graduate	4	5.9%
Bachelor's degree	9	13.2%
Graduate degree	8	11.8%
In college	35	51.1%
TOTAL	68	

Southern Accent?		
Yes	27	39.7%
No	41	60.3%
TOTAL	68	

Area of Kentucky		
Louisville	35	51.5%
Central Kentucky	18	26.5%
Northern Kentucky	3	4.4%
Eastern Kentucky	4	5.9%
Western Kentucky	0	0.0%
Omitted/not Kentucky	8	11.8%
TOTAL	68	

NOTES

CHAPTER 1

1. This inattention to linguistic borders and identity construction may be changing, however, as evidenced by a recent book titled *Language, Borders and Identity* (Watt and Llamas 2014) as well as a special issue of *Language and Communication* (Avineri and Kroskrity 2014).

2. For more information on Wolfram's projects, visit the North Carolina Language and Life Project website at http://www.ncsu.edu/linguistics/ncllp/.

3. Maps usually include state lines, as early studies (e.g., Preston 1989, 1993a) indicated that people have great difficulty with completely blank maps, due to a general lack of knowledge about American geography. The problem with this, however, is that respondents often "could not escape the notion that state lines were dialect boundaries, a fact which supports the conclusion that nonlinguists' impressions of the position of dialect boundaries are historical-political, not linguistic" (Preston 1989, 25). In all map drawing activities condutced within the project, only state lines appear.

4. Though perceptual and production maps often yield similar results, this need not be the case (Benson 2003).

5. This survey technique is an innovation in perceptual dialectology in several ways. First, instead of rating individual states on pleasantness, correctness, and degree of difference, as in most other studies in this research paradigm, participants rated the individual regions that they drew on their maps, allowing for greater insight as to why a particular label was selected and providing a true bottom-up approach to dialect perceptions. Also, the scale included categories beyond these traditional three, including other social characteristics popularly connected to speech (i.e., beauty, education). This modification provided a more nuanced understanding of the dialect areas participants hold in high esteem and those seen as least desirable on many different dimensions. The scale itself was limited to four points, unlike much of Preston (and others) previous work in this area, so as to discourage participants from selecting only the middle number for all characteristics. Finally, the inclusion of open-ended questions on these surveys provided qualitative data that was used in making categorizations in the data analysis.

6. Students with hometowns outside Kentucky were instructed to find people from the state. The goal was to get as many respondents from as many different portions of the state as possible.

7. SOAPnet, the now-defunct cable and satellite channel, was known for airing recent and older episodes of soap operas and primetime dramas, but it also occasionally produced original programming, including this and other reality-type shows.

8.   For more on reality television shows, their structure, and their popularity, see e.g., Biressi and Nunn (2005) and Murray and Ouellette (2009).

9.   *Louisville* is known for having many different pronunciations. Non-Louisvillians seem to have difficulty understanding one of these pronunciations, [ˈluːəvəl], often shortened to [ˈlʌvəl], which differs widely from the standard English pronunciation [ˈluːiːvɪl]. See Cramer (2013) for a discussion of the connection between pronunciation of *Louisville* and Southernness.

10.   In the case of the mergers data, 10–14 tokens of each vowel were selected. The reason for the variation has to do with the way in which words were selected from the corpus. All words that met the criteria were considered, but for many speakers this meant that the number was less than 10 unique root tokens. For each vowel, the first instance of each unique root was taken first, then the second instance alphabetically, and so on until reaching 10, unless it was deemed to be a repeat due to editing. For those speakers with more than 10 unique roots, all were kept for the analysis. Additionally, if sounds were not discernible due to overlapping speech or loss of initial sounds (like in *them*), the next token in the list was selected.

CHAPTER 2

1.   *Kentuckiana* is a portmanteau, or blending, of the two state names, *Kentucky* and *Indiana*.

2.   Class 1 cities have a population greater than 100,000. However, the numbers given in this report indicate that Lexington–Fayette County, in its postmerger status, may also have a large enough population to be classified as such. Since officials from Lexington have yet to seek reclassification, Louisville is still the only city in the state with the Class 1 distinction.

3.   The fact that most of the Ohio River is actually inside Kentucky's border has generated some controversy in state politics. For instance, Kentucky does not permit casino gambling but Indiana does, thus forcing Indiana casino boats that had once cruised the Ohio River to permanently dock because of Kentucky's control over the river.

4.   Later, the two papers merged to become the *Courier-Journal*, which is the current newspaper in the city.

5.   The way in which Louisville differs culturally from the rest of the state is similar to the way that Chicago is often considered to be different from the rest of Illinois. Bigham (2010) found that the Southern-Northern cultural divide in Illinois was so strong that it was reflected in their linguistic practices and attitudes, thus "helping to reify the 'Southern Illinois vs. Chicagoland' ideology" (194). While accommodation is not explicitly explored in this project as it was in Bigham's, my expectation is that similar results would be found.

CHAPTER 3

1. As in Fridland and Bartlett (2006), Alaska and Hawaii are included in a category called "Other," while New York City is included in calculations for the Upper North, and Washington, D.C., is included in calculations for the South.

2. Please note that when labels from individual maps are cited, the spelling, punctuation, and capitalization used by the participant have been retained. In all individual maps, a star has been added to mark the geographic location of Louisville. This marking was not, however, provided to participants.

3. As is clear from his map (figure 3.5), this participant did not exactly follow directions; however, regions that were shaded instead of circled were preserved in the digitization process by selecting the outermost edge of the shaded region and state lines as the bounding lines of the region. Additionally, because of time constraints, this participant was unable to provide language attitude data for all of the regions he delimited.

4. Language attitudes information was consulted as well, to assure the correct classification. For example, when participants linked a particular label to the speech of people who live in the mountains, this label was also subsumed under the "Appalachia" overarching category. A region was included in the composite map only if at least 14% of respondents included it on their maps.

5. Each of the individual regional maps includes all responses within that category. The darkest shading in the region is the area that was included in the most maps, while the lightest shaded regions represent only one selection. Additionally, even though respondents drew lines outside of the state boundaries provided in the test instrument, I have cropped the composite shaded portions to align with state lines, since it is unclear whether participants intended to indicate anything about the possible adjoining states.

6. See http://math.ucalgary.ca/files/math/tukey_table.pdf for a distribution table. For q, the distribution table is based on degrees of freedom of error (dfe) and number of treatments. Unfortunately, q distribution tables are not equipped to handle my data exactly. These tables list numbers of treatments up to ten, though my data from the regional map features 11 different groups. Additionally, the dfe listed in the tables includes 60 dfe and jumps up to 120 dfe, which did not match the dfe in any of my data sets. Thus, I chose conservatively within the chart. The critical value for the regional data was 4.65. For the Kentucky data, it was 3.92.

7. Then, as a precautionary measure, one more pairing was analyzed, to assure that no further significant values would be found. In the case of a tie in rank, the order of the analysis of the tied regions was based on highest number of responses selecting that label. In the case where the tied regions had the same number of responses, the analysis was done alphabetically. For example, in the correctness example above, the first pairing would be Appalachia and Chicago. But Chicago shares the number one ranking with Midwest, which also has the same number of responses. So the second pairing is Appalachia and Midwest.

This pairing procedure continues until the result produced by comparing Appalachia with some other region is not significant. Then, the second lowest ranked region, Cajun/Creole, with a mean score of 2.75, is compared to Chicago, then Midwest, and so on.

CHAPTER 4

1. What is more, because of the process I used in determining areas for digitization, Louisville and a couple other regions actually fall into both categories for this participant.

2. For the correctness and pleasantness task, participants were given a range of 1–10 for rating the states and two cities in this survey. For the degree of difference task, however, participants were only given a range of 1–4. This difference stems from earlier research in this domain (Niedzielski and Preston 2000).

3. This result is not in the table because a non–statistically significant result had already been discovered before this pairing took place. Their positions as number one and two in the rankings explains this lack of statistical significance.

4. The similarity to southern Indiana respondents in Preston's (1989) work is not surprising. The participants in that study come from the Indiana side of the Ohio River, just across from Louisville.

5. See Cramer (2013) for more on Louisvillians' thoughts about these first two stereotypes.

6. For our purposes, since the Louisville variety did not surface as its own variety in this study and since those regions that included only Louisville were determined by the author to be part of the Central Kentucky/Bluegrass region, this analysis will focus on how Louisvillians position that region with respect to the other regions in the state.

CHAPTER 5

1. Non-Louisvillians have not completed the regional map task. These data, therefore, cannot be discussed for non-Louisvillians. The focus in this chapter will be on data provided in the ratings of states and cities for level of correctness, pleasantness, and difference and on data provided in the Kentucky map project.

2. Such a factor is not easily quantifiable, as participants chose varying ways to align with a region. A simple count, for example, reveals that only three maps featured expressions such as "Like me" for any given region, all of which were from non-Louisville participants. Other ways of aligning included using more positive labels for their region than other groups used when referring to the same region, drawing smiley faces and hearts on regions that encompass their own hometown, among others, and such practices appear more common for non-Louisville participants.

3. Louisville data was also included in the production of this map.

4. Kentucky's tourism bureau, for example, puts Louisville in a region separate from Frankfort and Lexington. Louisville and surrounding towns are included in a region called "Bourbon, Horses & History," while Frankfort and Lexington (among other smaller towns) are included in the "Bluegrass Region." See http://www.kentuckytourism.com/ for more information.

5. A preliminary version of this analysis was presented in Cramer (2014).

6. It is possible, however, that many of these participants have reappropriated (Chen 1998) these terms for more acceptable use.

CHAPTER 6

1. The Back Shift is analyzed in this chapter, despite having been shown to be more widespread than being confined to the Southern dialect region, in order to be able to compare what earlier studies (e.g., Feagin 1986; Fridland 1998) have shown in relation to the SVS.

2. This merger is thought to be an unconditioned sound change (Labov, Ash, and Boberg 2006, 4), but it has been found to be transitional for some speakers, such that the distinction is neutralized in certain linguistic contexts before others (Thomas 2001). According to Hazen (2005), the merger happens first in the environment before /t/ and /k/, and these environments are the ones examined in this chapter.

3. While very few studies have presented acoustic analyses of reality television data, those that do have shown that these data are quite appropriate for phonetic and phonological analyses. Sonderegger (2012), for example, in exploring data from *Big Brother UK*, found that there is significant interaction between linguistic features, language users, and context of use in terms of linguistic variation, suggesting that there is a relationship between short-term shifts (like those that happen in conversation) and long-term ones (like those that occur across a person's lifetime). St-Amand (2012), who focuses on intraspeaker variation in Québécois French in Internet clips from *Occupation Double*, moved from phonetics to phonology by using the quantitative data collected from the show to investigate certain theoretical phonological phenomena. Further work with the *Southern Belles: Louisville* data could consider both exemplar influences on the phonology of the speech of these women and the possible role accommodation plays in the variation present.

4. In all analyses, F_1 and F_2 are considered separately.

5. The code for the Fibonacci line searches was adapted from Chong and Żak (2001).

6. The literature on monophthongs overwhelmingly defines them as consisting of a single steady-state with no transition. However, Hewlett and Beck (2006) claim that monophthongs and diphthongs are not discrete categories, but points on a continuum. Thus, vowels that are perceived to be monophthongs may exhibit a dynamic phase. My definition accounts for such monophthongs.

7. In Cramer (2009), I found some instances where either F_1 or F_2 but not both were monophthongal.

8. For individual utterances, which were taken from the transcript I created of the entire show, highlighted items indicate the word under examination. Items in square brackets indicate additional commentary.

9. In all of the examples presented in this section, our concern is primarily with the highlighted word, which is a word that has been presented in the previous section as quantitatively having monophthongal or diphthongal qualities. The context of the utterance of this word is presented to show whether the topic of discussion conditions the presence of a particular variant. It is interesting to note, however, that, at least anecdotally (i.e., in my cursory auditory examinations of the data), the monophthongal variant appears in contexts where several other /aɪ/ tokens also surface as monophthongs, but diphthongal variants tend to co-occur with both diphthongal and monophthongal variants.

REFERENCES

Allen, Harold B. 1973–76. *Linguistic Atlas of the Upper Midwest.* 3 vols. Minneapolis: University of Minnesota Press.

Alvarez, Robert R., Jr. 1995. "The Mexican-US Border: The Making of an Anthropology of Borderlands." *Annual Review of Anthropology* 24: 447–70. doi:10.1146/annurev.an.24.100195.002311.

Appadurai, Arjun. 1988. "Introduction: Place and Voice in Anthropological Theory." *Cultural Anthropology* 3.1: 16–20. doi:10.1525/can.1988.3.1.02a00020.

Ash, Sharon. 2006. "The North American Midland as a Dialect Area." In *Language Variation and Change in the American Midland: A New Look at "Heartland" English,* edited by Thomas E. Murray and Beth Lee Simon, 33–56. Amsterdam: Benjamins. doi:10.1075/veaw.g36.04ash.

Association of Religion Data Archive. 2010. "State Membership Report: Kentucky." http://www.thearda.com/rcms2010/r/s/21/rcms2010_21_state_adh_2010.asp. Based on data from *2010 U.S. Religion Census: Religious Congregations and Membership Study.* Kansas City, Mo.: Association of Statisticians of American Religious Bodies.

Atwood, E. Bagby. 1953. *A Survey of Verb Forms in the Eastern United States.* Ann Arbor: University of Michigan Press.

Avineri, Netta, and Paul V. Kroskrity. 2014. "On the (Re-)production and Representation of Endangered Language Communities: Social Boundaries and Temporal Borders." *Language and Communication* 38: 1–7. doi:10.1016/j.langcom.2014.05.003.

Bailey, Charles-James N. 1968. "Is There a 'Midland' Dialect of American English?" Paper presented at the 1968 summer meeting of the Linguistic Society of America, Urbana, Ill., July 25–26. http://eric.ed.gov/?id=ED021240.

Bailey, Guy. 1997. "When Did Southern American English Begin?" In *Englishes around the World: Studies in Honour of Manfred Görlach,* vol. 1, *General Studies, British Isles, North America,* edited by Edgar W. Schneider, 255–75. Amsterdam: Benjamins.

Bailey, Guy, Tom Wikle, Jan Tillery, and Lori Sand. 1993. "Some Patterns of Linguistic Diffusion." *Language Variation and Change* 5.3: 359–90. doi:10.1017/S095439450000154X.

Beach, Damian. 1995. *Civil War Battles, Skirmishes, and Events in Kentucky.* Louisville, Ky.: Different Drummer Books.

Bejarano, Cynthia L. 2006. *¿Qué onda? Urban Youth Culture and Border Identity.* Tucson: University of Arizona Press.

Bennett, Edward, and Carolyn Gatz. 2008. "A Restoring Prosperity Case Study: Louisville, Kentucky." Metropolitan Policy Program at Brookings. http://www.brookings.edu/research/papers/2008/09/17-louisville-bennett-gatz.

Benson, Erica J. 2003. "Folk Linguistic Perceptions and the Mapping of Dialect Boundaries." *American Speech* 78.3: 307–30. doi:10.1215/00031283-78-3-307.

Bhabha, Homi K. 1994. *The Location of Culture.* London: Routledge.

Bhatt, Rakesh M. 2008. "In Other Words: Language Mixing, Identity Representations, and *Third Space.*" *Journal of Sociolinguistics* 12.2: 177–200. doi:10.1111/j.1467-9841.2008.00363.x.

Bigham, Douglas S. 2010. "Mechanisms of Accommodation among Emerging Adults in a University Setting." *Journal of English Linguistics* 38.3: 193–210. doi:10.1177/0075424210373542.

Billings, Dwight B. 1999. "Introduction." In *Confronting Appalachian Stereotypes: Back Talk from an American Region,* edited by Dwight B. Billings, Gurney Norman, and Katherine Ledford, 3–20. Lexington: University Press of Kentucky.

Billings, Dwight B., Gurney Norman, and Katherine Ledford, eds. 1999. *Confronting Appalachian Stereotypes: Back Talk from an American Region.* Lexington: University Press of Kentucky.

Biressi, Anita, and Heather Nunn. 2005. *Reality TV: Realism and Revelation.* London: Wallflower.

Blake, Renee, Elizabeth Coggshall, Daniel Erker, and Michael Taylor. 2008. "New York City English: Perceptual Dialectology and Research Design." Paper presented at New Ways of Analyzing Variation 37, Houston, Texas, Nov. 6–9.

Bloomfield, Leonard. 1944. "Secondary and Tertiary Responses to Language." *Language* 20.2: 45–55. doi:10.2307/409893.

Boersma, Paul, and David Weenink. 2015. Praat: Doing Phonetics by Computer. Version 5.4.08. http://www.praat.org.

Bowie, David. 2000. "The Effect of Geographic Mobility on the Retention of a Local Dialect." Ph.D. diss., University of Pennsylvania.

Bucholtz, Mary. 1999. "'Why Be Normal?' Language and Identity Practices in a Community of Nerd Girls." *Language in Society* 28.2: 203–23. doi://10.1017/S0047404599002043.

Bucholtz, Mary, Nancy Bermudez, Victor Fung, Lisa Edwards, and Rosalva Vargas. 2007. "Hella Nor Cal or Totally So Cal? The Perceptual Dialectology of California." *Journal of English Linguistics* 35.4: 325–52. doi:10.1177/0075424207307780.

Bucholtz, Mary, Nancy Bermudez, Victor Fung, Rosalva Vargas, and Lisa Edwards. 2008. "The Normative North and the Stigmatized South: Ideology and Methodology in the Perceptual Dialectology of California." *Journal of English Linguistics* 36.1: 62–87. doi:10.1177/0075424207311721.

Bucholtz, Mary, and Kira Hall. 2004. "Language and Identity." In *A Companion to Linguistic Anthropology,* edited by Alessandro Duranti, 369–94. Malden, Mass.: Blackwell.

———. 2005. "Identity and Interaction: A Sociocultural Linguistic Approach." *Discourse Studies* 7.4–5: 585–614. doi:10.1177/1461445605054407.

Bustamante, Jorge A. 1978. "Commodity-Migrants: Structural Analysis of Mexican Immigration to the United States." In *Views across the Border: The United States and Mexico*, edited by Stanley R. Ross, 183–203. Albuquerque: University of New Mexico Press.

Carvalho, Ana Maria. 2006. "Spanish (s) Aspiration as a Prestige Marker on the Uruguayan-Brazilian Border." In "Language Variation and Change: Historical and Contemporary Perspectives," edited by Clare Mar-Molinero and Miranda Stewart. Special issue, *Spanish in Context* 3.1: 85–114. doi:10.1075/sic.3.1.07car.

———. 2010. "¿Eres De la Frontera O SOS De la Capital? Variation and Alternation of Second-Person Verbal Forms in Uruguayan Border Spanish." *Southwest Journal of Linguistics* 29.1: 1–23.

———. 2014. "Introduction: Towards a Sociolinguistics of the Border." *International Journal of the Sociology of Language* 227: 1–7. doi:10.1515/ijsl-2013-0084.

Carver, Craig M. 1987. *American Regional Dialects: A Word Geography*. Ann Arbor: University of Michigan Press.

Chambers, J. K., and Peter Trudgill. 1980. *Dialectology*. Cambridge: Cambridge University Press.

Chen, Melinda Yuen-Ching. 1998. "'I am an Animal!' Lexical Reappropriation, Performativity, and Queer." In *Engendering Communication: Proceedings from the Fifth Berkeley Women and Language Conference*, edited by Suzanne Wertheim, Ashlee C. Bailey, and Monica Corston-Oliver, 129–40. Berkeley, Calif.: Berkeley Women and Language Group.

Chong, Edwin K. P., and Stanislaw H. Żak. 2001. *An Introduction to Optimization*. 2nd ed. New York: Wiley.

City-Data.com. 2007. "Kentucky…specifically Louisville…south or midwest?" City-Data Forum. http://www.city-data.com/forum/louisville-area/85418-kentucky-specificallylouisville-south-midwest.html.

Coupland, Nikolas, Angie Williams, and Peter Garrett. 1999. "'Welshness' and 'Englishness' as Attitudinal Dimensions of English Language Varieties in Wales." In *Handbook of Perceptual Dialectology*, vol. 1, edited by Dennis R. Preston, 333–43. Amsterdam: Benjamins. doi:10.1075/z.hpd1.28cou.

Courier-Journal (Louisville, Ky.). 2009. "The Derby: It's More Than a Horse Race." May 2.

Cramer, Jennifer. 2009. "Steady-state Patterns of /ai/ in Southern and Midland Dialects: The Case of Louisville." Paper presented at the annual meeting of the Linguistic Society of America, San Francisco, Calif., Jan. 8–11.

———. 2011. "Perceiving Appalachia: A Perspective from the City." Paper presented at the Southeastern Conference on Linguistics 78, Pine Mountain, Ga., Apr. 13–15.

———. 2012. "Is Kentucky Midwestern? Two Mergers Reveal Marginality" Paper presented as part of a panel on the sociophonetics of Midwest English at New Ways of Analyzing Variation 41, Bloomington, Ind., Oct. 25–28.

———. 2013. "Styles, Stereotypes, and the South: Constructing Identities at the Linguistic Border." *American Speech* 88.2: 144–67. doi:10.1215/00031283-2346753.

————. 2014. "Appalachian Folk Beliefs and Language Variation in Kentucky." Paper presented at the Southeastern Conference on Linguistics 81, Myrtle Beach, S.C., Mar. 27–29.

————. 2015a. "Country vs. 'Country': Using Punctuation to Mediate Negative Perceptions in Labeling Appalachian Speech." Paper presented at the Southeastern Conference on Linguistics 82, Raleigh, N.C., Apr. 9–11.

————. 2015b. "An Optimality-Theoretic Approach to Dialect Code-Switching." *English World-Wide* 36.2: 170–97. doi:10.1075/eww.36.2.02cra.

————. 2016. "Rural vs. Urban: Perception and Production of Identity in a Border City." In *Cityscapes and Perceptual Dialectology: Global Perspectives on Non-linguists' Knowledge of the Dialect Landscape*, edited by Jennifer Cramer and Chris Montgomery, 27–53. Berlin: Mouton de Gruyter.

Cramer, Jennifer, and Chris Montgomery, eds. 2016. *Cityscapes and Perceptual Dialectology: Global Perspectives on Non-linguists' Knowledge of the Dialect Landscape*. Language and Social Life 5. Berlin: Mouton de Gruyter.

Dakin, Robert F. 1971. "South Midland Speech in the Old Northwest." *Journal of English Linguistics* 5: 31–48. doi:10.1177/007542427100500103.

DARE. Dictionary of American Regional English. 1985–2013. Edited by Frederic G. Cassidy and Joan Houston Hall. 6 vols. Cambridge, Mass.: Belknap Press of Harvard University Press. Available electronically at http://www.daredictionary.com/.

Davis, Lawrence M., and Charles L. Houck. 1992. "Is There a Midland Dialect Area?—Again." *American Speech* 67.1: 61–70. doi:10.2307/455758.

de García, Kati Pletsch. 2006. "¡Ala! Linguistic Innovation and the Blending of Cultures on the South Texas Border." *Southwest Journal of Linguistics* 27.1: 1–15.

Demirci, Mahide, and Brian Kleiner. 1999. "The Perception of Turkish Dialects." In *Handbook of Perceptual Dialectology*, vol. 1, edited by Dennis R. Preston, 263–81. Amsterdam: Benjamins. doi:10.1075/z.hpd1.25dem.

Diercks, Willy. 2002. "Mental Maps: Linguistic-Geographic Concepts." In *Handbook of Perceptual Dialectology*, vol. 2, edited by Daniel Long and Dennis R. Preston, 51–70. Amsterdam: Benjamins. doi:10.1075/z.hpd2.10die.

Emporis.com. 2015. "Louisville." http://www.emporis.com/city/101641/louisville-ky-usa (accessed June 25).

Evans, Betsy E. 2011. "'Seattletonian' to 'Faux Hick': Perceptions of English in Washington State." *American Speech* 86.4: 383–413. doi:10.1215/00031283-1587232.

————. 2013. "'Everybody Sounds the Same': Otherwise Overlooked Ideology in Perceptual Dialectology." *American Speech* 88.1: 63–80. doi:10.1215/00031283-2322637.

Feagin, Crawford. 1986. "More Evidence for Vowel Change in the South." In *Diversity and Diachrony*, edited by David Sankoff, 83–95. Amsterdam: Benjamins.

————. 2000. "Sound Change in the South." *American Speech* 75.4: 342–44. doi:10.1215/00031283-75-4-342.

Findling, John E. 2009. *Louisville*. Charleston, S.C.: Arcadia Publishing.

Flynn, Donna K. 1997. "'We Are the Border': Identity, Exchange, and the State along the Bénin-Nigeria Border." *American Ethnologist* 24.2: 311–30. doi:10.1525/ae .1997.24.2.311.

Frazer, Timothy C. 1994. "On Transition Areas and the 'Midland' Dialect: A Reply to Davis and Houck." *American Speech* 69.4: 430–35. doi:10.2307/455861.

———. 1996. "The Dialects of the Middle West." In *Focus on the USA: Varieties of English Around the World*, edited by Edgar W. Schneider, 81–102. Amsterdam: Benjamins.

Fridland, Valerie. 1998. "The Southern Vowel Shift: Linguistic and Social Factors." Ph.D. diss., Michigan State University.

———. 2000. "The Southern Shift in Memphis, Tennessee." *Language Variation and Change* 11.3: 267–85. doi:10.1017/S0954394599113024.

———. 2001. "The Social Dimension of the Southern Vowel Shift: Gender, Age and Class." *Journal of Sociolinguistics* 5.2: 233–53. doi:10.1111/1467-9481.00149.

Fridland, Valerie, and Kathryn Bartlett. 2006. "Correctness, Pleasantness, and Degree of Difference Ratings across Regions." *American Speech* 81.4: 358–86. doi:10.1215/00031283-2006-025.

Fridland, Valerie, Kathryn Bartlett, and Roger Kreuz. 2005. "Making Sense of Variation: Pleasantness and Education Ratings of Southern Vowel Variants." *American Speech* 80.4: 366–87. doi:10.1215/00031283-80-4-366.

Galasiński, Dariusz, and Ulrike H. Meinhof. 2002. "Looking across the River: German-Polish Border Communities and the Construction of the Other." *Journal of Language and Politics* 1.1: 23–58. doi:10.1075/jlp.1.1.05gal.

Giles, Howard. 1970. "Evaluative Reactions to Accents." *Educational Review* 22.3: 211–27. doi:10.1080/0013191700220301.

Giles, Howard, Richard Bourhis, and Ann Davies. 1979. "Prestige Speech Styles: The Imposed Norm and Inherent Value Hypotheses." In *Language and Society: Anthropological Issues*, edited by Willilam C. McCormack and Stephen A. Wurm, 589–96. The Hague: Mouton.

Gordon, Matthew J. 2006. "Tracking the Low Back Merger in Missouri." In *Language Variation and Change in the American Midland: A New Look at "Heartland" English*, edited by Thomas E. Murray and Beth Lee Simon, 57–68. Amsterdam: Benjamins. doi:10.1075/veaw.g36.05gor.

Gould, Peter, and Rodney White. 1986. *Mental Maps*. 2nd ed. Boston: Allen and Unwin.

Hansen, Niles M. 1981. *The Border Economy: Regional Development in the Southwest*. Austin: University of Texas Press.

Harkins, Anthony. 2015. "Colonels, Hillbillies, and Fightin': Twentieth-Century Kentucky in the National Imagination." *Register of the Kentucky Historical Society* 113.2–3: 421–52. doi:10.1353/khs.2015.0043.

Hartley, Laura C. 1999. "A View from the West: Perceptions of U.S. Dialects by Oregon Residents." In *Handbook of Perceptual Dialectology*, vol. 1, edited by Dennis R. Preston, 315–32. Amsterdam: Benjamins. doi:10.1075/z.hpd1.27har.

Hazen, Kirk. 2002. "Identity and Language Variation in a Rural Community." *Language* 78.2: 240–57. http://www.jstor.org/stable/3086557.

———. 2005. "Mergers in the Mountains: West Virginia Division and Unification." *English World-Wide* 26.2: 199–221. doi:10.1075/eww.26.2.05haz.

Hewlett, Nigel, and Janet Beck. 2006. *An Introduction to the Science of Phonetics.* Mahwah, N.J.: Lawrence Erlbaum.

Hillenbrand, James, Laura A. Getty, Michael J. Clark, and Kimberlee Wheeler. 1995. "Acoustic Characteristics of American English Vowels." *Journal of the Acoustical Society of America* 97.5: 3099–111. doi:10.1121/1.411872.

Hoenigswald, Henry M. 1966. "A Proposal for the Study of Folk-Linguistics." In *Sociolinguistics: Proceedings of the UCLC Sociolinguistics Conference, 1964,* edited by William Bright, 16–26. The Hague: Mouton.

Holmes, Janet. 1997. "Women, Language and Identity." *Journal of Sociolinguistics* 1.2: 195–223. doi:10.1111/1467-9481.00012.

Howren, Robert. 1958. "The Speech of Louisville, Kentucky." Ph.D. diss., Indiana University.

Hulbert, Archer Butler. 1903. *Boone's Wilderness Road.* Cleveland, Ohio: Arthur H. Clark.

Irons, Terry Lynn. 2007. "On the Southern Shift in Appalachian English." In "Selected Papers from NWAV 35," edited by Toni Cook and Keelan Evanini. *University of Pennsylvania Working Papers in Linguistics* 13.2: 121–34. http://repository.upenn.edu/pwpl/vol13/iss2/10.

Irvine, Judith T., and Susan Gal. 2000. "Language Ideology and Linguistic Differentiation." In *Regimes of Language: Ideologies, Politics, and Identities,* edited by Paul V. Kroskrity, 35–84. Santa Fe, N.M.: School of American Research Press.

Johnson, Ellen. 1994. "Yet Again: The Midland Dialect." *American Speech* 69.4: 419–30. doi:10.2307/455860.

Johnstone, Barbara. 2004. "Place, Globalization, and Linguistic Variation." In *Sociolinguistic Variation: Critical Reflections,* edited by Carmen Fought, 65–83. Oxford: Oxford University Press.

José, Brian. 2010. "Historical and Contemporary Influences on Regional Dialect Variation in Two Indiana Communities Bordering the American Midland." Paper presented at the Borders and Identities Conference, Newcastle-upon-Tyne, U.K., Jan. 8–9.

Kentucky League of Cities. 2011. "KLC Research Report: The Basics of Kentucky Cities." http://www.klc.org/UserFiles/TheBasics2011_Sept(2).pdf.

Kentucky State Board of Elections. 2004. "2004 Primary and General Election Results." http://elect.ky.gov/results/2000-2009/Pages/2004primaryandgeneral electionresults.aspx.

Kleber, John E., ed. 2001. *The Encyclopedia of Louisville.* Lexington: University Press of Kentucky.

Kretzschmar, William A., Jr. 2004. "Linguistics Atlas Projects." http://us.english.uga.edu/.

Kroskrity, Paul V. 2004. "Language Ideologies." In *A Companion to Linguistic Anthropology*, edited by Alessandro Duranti, 496–517. Malden, Mass.: Blackwell.

Kroskrity, Paul V., and Netta Avineri, eds. 2014. "Reconceptualizing Endangered Language Communities: Crossing Borders and Constructing Boundaries." Special issue, *Language and Communication* 38.

Kuiper, Lawrence. 1999. "Variation and the Norm: Parisian Perceptions of Regional France." In *Handbook of Perceptual Dialectology*, vol. 1, edited by Dennis R. Preston, 243–62. Amsterdam: Benjamins. doi:10.1075/z.hpd1.24kui.

Kurath, Hans. 1949. *A Word Geography of the Eastern United States*. Ann Arbor: University of Michigan Press.

Kurath, Hans, Miles L. Hanley, Bernard Bloch, Guy S. Lowman, Jr., and Marcus L. Hansen. 1939–43. *Linguistic Atlas of New England*. 3 vols. Providence, R.I.: Brown University.

Kurath, Hans, and Raven I. McDavid, Jr. 1961. *The Pronunciation of English in the Atlantic States: Based upon the Collections of the Linguistic Atlas of the Eastern United States*. Ann Arbor: University of Michigan Press.

Labov, William. 1972. *Sociolinguistic Patterns*. Oxford: Blackwell.

———. 1991. "The Three Dialects of English." In *New Ways of Analyzing Sound Change*, edited by Penelope Eckert, 1–44. New York: Academic Press.

———. 1996. "The Organization of Dialect Diversity in North America." Paper presented at the Fourth International Conference on Spoken Language Processing, Philadelphia, Pa., Oct. 3–6. Revised version available at http://www.ling.upenn.edu/phono_atlas/ICSLP4.html.

———. 2010. *Principles of Linguistic Change*. Vol. 3, *Cognitive and Cultural Factors*. Chichester, U.K.: Wiley-Blackwell.

Labov, William, Sharon Ash, and Charles Boberg. 2006. *The Atlas of North American English: Phonetics, Phonology and Sound Change, a Multimedia Reference Tool*. Berlin: Mouton de Gruyter.

Lehiste, Ilse, and Gordon E. Peterson. 1961. "Transitions, Glides, and Diphthongs." *Journal of the Acoustical Society of America* 33: 268–77. doi:10.1121/1.1908638.

Le Page, R. B., and Andrée Tabouret-Keller. 1985. *Acts of Identity: Creole-Based Approaches to Language and Ethnicity*. Cambridge: Cambridge University Press.

Llamas, Carmen. 2007. "'A Place between Places': Language and Identities in a Border Town." *Language in Society* 36.4: 579–604. doi:10.1017/S0047404507070455.

Long, Daniel, and Young-Cheol Yim. 2002. "Regional Differences in the Perception of Korean Dialects." In *Handbook of Perceptual Dialectology*, vol. 2, edited by Daniel Long and Dennis R. Preston, 249–75. Amsterdam: Benjamins. doi:10.1075/z.hpd2.19lon.

Long, Daniel, and Dennis R. Preston, eds. 2002. *Handbook of Perceptual Dialectology*. Vol. 2. Amsterdam: Benjamins. doi:10.1075/z.hpd2.

Louisville Metro Government. 2009. "Louisville Metro Government Website." http://www.louisvilleky.gov/.

Louisville–Southern Indiana Ohio River Bridges Project. 2013. "The Ohio River Bridges." http://www.kyinbridges.com/.

McDavid, Raven I., Jr., and Raymond O'Cain, eds. 1980. *Linguistic Atlas of the Middle and South Atlantic States*. Chicago: University of Chicago Press.

McMeekin, Isabel McLennan. 1946. *Louisville: The Gateway City*. New York: J. Messner.

Meyer, David R. 1989. "Midwestern Industrialization and the American Manufacturing Belt in the Nineteenth Century." *Journal of Economic History* 49.4: 921–37. doi:10.1017/S0022050700009505.

Miller, Daniel A. 2008. "Discovering the Quantity of Quality: Scoring 'Regional Identity' for Quantitative Research." *Language Sciences* 30.6: 652–78. doi:10.1016/j.langsci.2006.09.003.

Milroy, Lesley 1980. *Language and Social Networks*. Baltimore, Md.: University Park Press.

———. 2004. "Language Ideologies and Linguistic Change." In *Sociolinguistic Variation: Critical Reflections*, edited by Carmen Fought, 161–77. Oxford: Oxford University Press.

Mishoe, Margaret. 1995. "Dialect Code-Switching among Lower Class Socioeconomic Speakers in the Southern United States: A Sociolinguistic Study." Ph.D. diss., University of South Carolina.

Moreno Fernández, Juliana, and Francisco Moreno Fernández. 2002. "Madrid Perceptions of Regional Varieties in Spain." In *Handbook of Perceptual Dialectology*, vol. 2, edited by Daniel Long and Dennis R. Preston, 295–320. Amsterdam: Benjamins. doi:10.1075/z.hpd2.21mor.

Montgomery, Chris. 2007. "Northern English Dialects: A Perceptual Approach." Ph.D. diss., University of Sheffield.

———. 2012. "The Effect of Proximity in Perceptual Dialectology." *Journal of Sociolinguistics* 16.5: 638–68. doi:10.1111/josl.12003.

Montgomery, Chris, and Philipp Stoeckle. 2013. "Geographic Information Systems and Perceptual Dialectology: A Method for Processing Draw-a-Map Data." *Journal of Linguistic Geography* 1.1: 52–85. doi:10.1017/jlg.2013.4.

Murray, Susan, and Laurie Ouellette, eds. 2009. *Reality TV: Remaking Television Culture*. 2nd ed. New York: New York University Press.

Negrón, Rosalyn. 2014. "New York City's Latino Ethnolinguistic Repertoire and the Negotiation of Latinidad in Conversation." *Journal of Sociolinguistics* 18.1: 87–118. doi:10.1111/josl.12063.

Niedzielski, Nancy A., and Dennis R. Preston. 2000. *Folk Linguistics*. Berlin: Mouton de Gruyter.

Pederson, Lee, Susan McDaniel, and Carol Adams. 1986–92. *Linguistic Atlas of the Gulf States*. 7 vols. Athens: University of Georgia Press.

Peterson, Gordon E., and Harold L. Barney. 1952. "Control Methods Used in a Study of the Vowels." *Journal of the American Acoustical Society of America* 24: 175–84. doi:10.1121/1.1906875.

Preston, Dennis R. 1989. *Perceptual Dialectology: Nonlinguists' Views of Areal Linguistics.* Dordrecht: Foris.

———. 1993a. "Folk Dialectology." In *American Dialect Research,* edited by Dennis R. Preston, 333–77. Amsterdam: Benjamins. doi:10.1075/z.68.17pre.

———. 1993b. "The Uses of Folk Linguistics." *International Journal of Applied Linguistics* 3.2: 181–259. doi:10.1111/j.1473-4192.1993.tb00049.x.

———, ed. 1999. *Handbook of Perceptual Dialectology.* Vol. 1. Amsterdam: Benjamins.

Preston, Dennis R., and George M. Howe. 1987. "Computerized Studies of Mental Dialect Maps." In *Variation in Language: NWAV-XV at Stanford; Proceedings of the Fifteenth Annual Conference on New Ways of Analyzing Variation,* edited by Keith M. Denning, Sharon Inkelas, John R. Rickford, and Faye C. McNair-Knox, 361–78. Stanford, Calif.: Department of Linguistics, Stanford University.

Regional Plan Association. 2013. "Great Lakes." http://www.america2050.org/great_lakes.html.

Rensink, W. G. 1955. "Dialectindeling naar Opgaven van Medewerkers." *Mededelingen der Centrale Commissie voor Onderzoek van het Nederlandse Volkseigen* 7: 20–23. Translated as "Informant Classification of Dialects" in *Handbook of Perceptual Dialectology,* vol. 1, edited by Dennis R. Preston, 3–7. Amsterdam: Benjamins, 1999. doi:10.1075/z.hpd1.07ren.

Romanello, Maria Teresa. 2002. "The Perception of Urban Varieties: Preliminary Studies from the South of Italy." In *Handbook of Perceptual Dialectology,* vol. 2, edited by Daniel Long and Dennis R. Preston, 329–49. Amsterdam: Benjamins. doi:10.1075/z.hpd2.23rom.

Rosaldo, Renato. 1988. "Ideology, Place, and People without Culture." *Cultural Anthropology* 3.1: 77–87. doi:10.1525/can.1988.3.1.02a00070.

———. 1993. *Culture and Truth: The Remaking of Social Analysis.* Boston: Beacon Hill.

Sandøy, Helge. 2011. "Language Culture in Norway: A Tradition of Questioning Standard Language Norms." In *Standard Language and Language Standards in a Changing Europe,* edited by Tore Kristiansen and Nikolas Coupland, 119–26. Oslo: Novus Press.

Share, Allen J. 1982. *Cities in the Commonwealth: Two Centuries of Urban Life in Kentucky.* Lexington: University Press of Kentucky.

Sibata, Takesi (柴田武). 1959. "方言境界の意識."「言語研究」36: 1–30. Translated as "Consciousness of Dialect Boundaries" by Daniel Long in *Handbook of Perceptual Dialectology,* vol. 1, edited by Dennis R. Preston, 39–62. Amsterdam: Benjamins, 1999. doi:10.1075/z.hpd1.11sib.

Silverstein, Michael. 1979. "Language Structure and Linguistic Ideology." In *The Elements: A Parasession on Linguistic Units and Levels, April 20–21, 1979,* edited by Paul R. Clyne, William F. Hanks, and Carol L. Hofbauer, 193–247. Chicago: Chicago Linguistic Society.

SkyscraperPage.com. 2008. "Louisville Southern or Midwestern (Southern Edition). SkyscraperPage.com forum." http://forum.skyscraperpage.com/showthread.php?t=162001.

SOAPnet. 2009. "Soapnet's New Original Docusoap, 'Southern Belles: Louisville,' Premieres Thursday, May 21 at 10:00 PM ET/PT." Press release. https://web .archive.org/web/20090429051955/http://www.soapnetmedianet.com/ web/showpage/showpage.aspx?program_id=3118697&type=lead.

Sonderegger, Morgan. 2012. "Phonetic and Phonological Dynamics on Reality Television." Ph.D. diss., University of Chicago.

Southern Belles: Louisville. 2009. Executive producers Joe Livecchi, Donald Bull, and R. Greg Johnson. 10 episodes (May 21–July 23). SOAPnet.

St-Amand, Anne-Bridget. 2012. "Hiatus and Hiatus Resolution in Québécois French." Ph.D. diss., University of Toronto.

Stevens, Kenneth N. 1998. *Acoustic Phonetics.* Cambridge, Mass.: MIT Press.

Stoddard, Ellwyn R., Richard L. Nostrand, and Jonathan P. West, eds. 1982. *Borderlands Sourcebook: A Guide to the Literature on Northern Mexico and the American Southwest.* Norman: University of Oklahoma Press.

Tenkotte, Paul A., and James C. Claypool, eds. 2009. *The Encyclopedia of Northern Kentucky.* Lexington: University Press of Kentucky.

Thomas, Erik R. 2000. "Spectral Differences in /ai/ Offsets Conditioned by Voicing of the Following Consonant." *Journal of Phonetics* 28.1: 1–25. doi:10.1006/ jpho.2000.0103.

———. 2001. *An Acoustic Analysis of Vowel Variation in New World English.* Publication of the American Dialect Society 85. Durham, N.C.: Duke University Press.

———. 2008. "Rural Southern White Accents." In *Varieties of English,* vol. 2, *The Americas and the Caribbean,* edited by Edgar W. Schneider, 87–114. Berlin: Mouton de Gruyter. doi:10.1515/9783110208405.1.87.

———. 2010. "A Longitudinal Analysis of the Durability of the Northern-Midland Dialect Boundary in Ohio." *American Speech* 85.4: 375–430. doi:10.1215/0003 1283-2010-022.

Trudgill, Peter, and Howard Giles. 1978. "Sociolinguistics and Linguistic Value Judgments: Correctness, Adequacy, and Aesthetics." In *Functional Studies in Language and Literature,* edited by Frank Coppieters and Didier L. Goyvaerts, 167–90. Gent: Story-Scientia.

Turner, Frederick Jackson. 1911. "The Place of the Ohio Valley in American History." *Ohio Archæological and Historical Quarterly* 20.1: 32–47. Reprinted as "The Ohio Valley in American History" in *History Teacher's Magazine* 2.7 (Mar. 1911): 147–52.

U.S. Bureau of Economic Analysis. 2011. "Percent Change in Real GDP by State, 2011. Bureau of Economic Analysis." http://www.bea.gov/newsreleases/regional/gdp _state/2012/_images/gsp_0612.png.

U.S. Census Bureau. 2013. "Metropolitan and Micropolitan – Delineation Files – People and Households." http://www.census.gov/population/metro/data/ def.html.

U.S. Department of Agriculture. 2014. "Corn for Grain 2014: Production by County for Selected States." http://www.nass.usda.gov/Charts_and_Maps/Crops_County/ pdf/CR-PR14-RGBChor.pdf.

U.S. Office of Management and Budget. 1974. "Standard Federal Regions." Circular A-105.

Watt, Dominic, and Carmen Llamas, eds. 2014. *Language, Borders and Identity.* Edinburgh: Edinburgh University Press.

Weijnen, Antonius A. 1946. "De grenzen tussen de Oost-Noordbrabantse dialecten onderling" [The borders between the dialects of eastern North Brabant]. In *Oost-Noordbrabantse dialectproblemen* [Eastern North Brabant dialect problems], edited by Antonius A. Weijnen, J. M. Renders, and Jac van Ginneken, 1–15. Amsterdam: Noord Hollandsche Uitgevers Maatschappij.

Williams, Cratis D. 1992. *Southern Mountain Speech.* Berea, Ky.: Berea College Press.

Wolfram, Walt. 2003. "Language Variation in the American South: An Introduction." *American Speech* 78.2: 123–29. doi:10.1215/00031283-78-2-123.

Wolfram, Walt, and Natalie Shilling-Estes. 2006. *American English: Dialects and Variation.* 2nd ed. Malden, Mass.: Blackwell.

Woolard, Kathryn A. 1992. "Language Ideology: Issues and Approaches." In "Language Ideologies," edited by Bambi B. Schieffelin, Paul V. Kroskrity, and Kathryn A. Woolard. Special issue, *Pragmatics* 2.3: 235–49. doi:10.1075/prag.2.3.01woo.

———. 2008. "Why *Dat* Now? Linguistic-Anthropological Contributions to the Explanation of Sociolinguistic Icons and Change." *Journal of Sociolinguistics* 12.4: 432–52. doi:10.1111/j.1467-9841.2008.00375.x.

Yater, George. 2001. "Louisville: A Historical Overview." In *The Encyclopedia of Louisville,* edited by John E. Kleber, xv–xxxi. Lexington: University Press of Kentucky.

Zwickl, Simone. 2002. *Language Attitudes, Ethnic Identity and Dialect Use across the Northern Ireland Border: Armagh and Monaghan.* Belfast: Queen's University.

INDEX